How to Get a Job in the Music and Recording Industry

By: Keith Hatschek

Editors: Kristen Schilo and Susan Gedutis

Berklee Press

Director: Dave Kusek
Managing Editor: Debbie Cavalier
Marketing Manager: Ola Frank
Sr. Writer/Editor: Jonathan Feist
Writer/Editor: Susan Gedutis
Product Manager: Ilene Altman

ISBN 0-634-01868-x

1140 Boylston Street
Boston, MA 02215-3693 USA
(617) 747-2146

Visit Berklee Press Online at
www.berkleepress.com

DISTRIBUTED BY

HAL•LEONARD®
CORPORATION
7777 W. BLUEMOUND RD. P.O. BOX 13819
MILWAUKEE, WISCONSIN 53213

Visit Hal Leonard Online at
www.halleonard.com

Contents

contents

Foreword

By Tony Brown,
President of MCA Records, Nashville

MCA Records Nashville President Tony Brown has left an indelible mark on the modern country sound. Throughout his career, he has worked with an incredible range of artists, including: Emmylou Harris, Vince Gill, Jimmy Buffet, Elvis Presley, Wynonna, Lyle Lovett, George Strait, Alabama, Shirley Caesar, Rosanne Cash, Rodney Crowell, The Mavericks, Reba McEntire, and Trisha Yearwood. Since he joined MCA in 1984, he has guided the company to its position as the number one label in Nashville in the 1990s. He has been awarded Billboard *magazine's coveted Top Country Producer honor seven times. Through it all, he has retained his reverence for great performers, a wonder for the "magic" in melody, and the simple joy of making music.*

When I started playing piano professionally more than thirty years ago with the Stamps Quartet, if a person had come up to me after a performance and predicted that I'd be the president of a record company one day, I would have replied, "Not in a million years!"

At the age of thirteen, I got my first glimpse of the life I wanted when gospel groups like the Statesmen and the Blackwood Brothers mesmerized me. The performers wore flashy clothes and drew huge audiences that they left cheering for more at the end of the night. To me, they were just like movie stars. It was then that I decided that I wanted a career in entertainment.

I started to play piano with a number of local gospel groups and began meeting the people who have helped me build my career. Meeting J.D. Sumner of the Blackwood Brothers forged one of the first links in my "chain," the people and the relationships that have opened doors for me. J.D. introduced me to a number of important people and eventually helped me land a gig as piano player for Elvis Presley in 1974.

As I worked with Elvis, that relationship led me from playing gospel music to country music. When Elvis died three years later in 1977, his previous piano player was leaving Emmylou Harris's band, and recommended me as his replacement. Soon my chain grew to include Emmylou, Ricky Skaggs, Vince Gill, Rodney Crowell, and Rosanne Cash, each of whom influenced my career tremendously. Constantly striving to meet and work with people more talented than me helped me learn and grow. I believe that I learned so much because my eyes and ears were wide open, and I was soaking up every bit of knowledge I could.

However, today, I've noticed that many young people aspiring to a career in the music business tend to remain in small circles of friends, and as a result, their world becomes very limited. From my point of view, the only way to succeed and enjoy this business is to enjoy all of it. You've got to constantly work to expand your universe.

Another important attribute to develop is self-assurance: learn to trust your vision and instincts. When Jimmy Bowen invited me to join him at MCA in 1984, he asked me if I had a vision that I wanted to achieve. I told him that, yes, I wanted to bring the amazing talent of instrumentalists like Mark O'Connor, Edgar Meyer, and John Jarvis to the public. These were session players I hung out with and played with every day, but they were completely unknown outside of Nashville.

I put a proposal together and soon, MCA's Master Series was born. The Master Series allowed me the opportunity to collaborate with a tremendous range of jazz, classical, and pop artists with whom I might have never worked. And it proved so successful that eventually MCA merged it with a larger jazz label, GRP. The impact of the Master Series on the artists involved has been long lasting. Just recently Edgar Meyer performed for an audience of millions with cellist Yo-Yo Ma on the 2000 Grammy telecast.

To bring the Master Series from a dream to a reality, I had to trust myself to know the difference between something that's really good versus something that's mediocre. There were times when I felt that I was in way over my head, but I realized I just had to keep my ears open and keep asking questions.

As I've made transitions from musician to producer to record company executive, a number of other skills have helped me to succeed. Being aware of what's happening around you, always remembering to follow up, developing the skill to really listen to people, and working to keep up with the trends and technologies shaping the music business are all critical skills that have to be practiced constantly.

You should take advantage of the people around you who can teach and help you expand your world. Keep your vision focused on what you want to do and make the most of every opportunity. Take the information in this book and combine it with your own creative abilities, and you've got the makings for a great career in the music business.

Tony Brown
Nashville, TN

Acknowledgements

The impetus to share my ideas on what it takes to launch a successful career in the music and recording industry came more than ten years ago. I found myself fielding a regular stream of calls from colleagues and acquaintances asking me to speak with a relative or friend who "wanted to get into the business." A few years later, my friend, entertainment attorney Marc Greenberg, and I were talking about what things we would still like to accomplish in our careers and I mentioned teaching. Shortly thereafter, he introduced me to the program director of the San Francisco State University Music and Recording Industry program, Mary Pieratt, and I have enjoyed lecturing there now for the past six years. Josh Hecht and John Altmann, who also teach recording arts, generously answered my numerous questions as I learned to become an effective teacher. My students have also stimulated and challenged me by asking difficult questions. They continually surprise me with their resourcefulness.

Since the day in 1965 when my first guitar—a red Orpheus with a chrome pick guard, three pickups, and a whammy bar—captivated me, I've had the good fortune to travel an always evolving road in the music and recording industry. My journey has been one of enlightenment and friendship shared with so many colleagues that it would be impossible to name each one. But I wish to especially thank David Porter for believing in me early in my career and for teaching me a great deal about what it takes to succeed in any business; Bruce Merley for sharing his balanced outlook on life and business when it has been most needed and for offering constructive criticism to an early draft of this book; Carson Taylor and Jim Treulich for instilling in me the need to aim high; and Roger Wiersema for helping provide "training wheels" and friendship to a journeyman engineer.

I am indebted to Richard A. Payne and his excellent volume, *How to Get a Better Job Quicker*. Mr. Payne's book has provided me with an excellent guide in my own career development. The volume provides any job seeker with a very complete and highly detailed presentation on successful resume development, salary negotiations, interviewing, and many other aspects of career development. It represents an excellent investment for any job seeker, regardless of their field of interest.

As my career grew, I was fortunate enough to become acquainted with a number of recording studio sages through the Society of Professional Audio Recording Services (SPARS)... Murray Allen, Tom Kobayashi, Chris Stone, Nick Colleran, Guy Costa, and Shirley Kaye... thank you for sharing so many of your insights. This same crew also taught me that when one has friends in the industry, access to a wealth of knowledge and experience capable of solving almost any problem is only a phone call away.

When I shifted gears and launched my agency, I was fortunate to tap the wisdom and wit of outstanding mentors Peter Weiglin, Marc Greenberg, and Al Rose. I hope I retain a fraction of the knowledge you have shared with me.

Hats off to my publishing team at Berklee Press, including David Kusek, Ola Frank, and Ilene Altman. Thanks to Kristen Schilo and Sue Gedutis for outstanding editing that shaped the words that worked so well in a lecture hall into a cohesive manuscript. Thanks to Jonathan Feist for his early advice and belief in the workshops and other key elements that have expanded and improved this work. Special thanks to Debbie Cavalier for her enthusiasm from the very beginning.

Without the patience, encouragement, and support of my family, Laura, Elyse, and Megan, this book would still be just an idea simmering on the back burner of my brain. And thanks to my parents, Helene and Hans Hatschek, who taught me the power of communication and the importance of love.

Keith Hatschek
San Francisco, California
December 2000

Introduction

You have likely purchased this book to find out what kinds of jobs exist in the music and recording industry. Or, you've already made a decision and know that working in one of the fields relating to "the business" is for you. But, where do you start to prepare for your career planning and job search?

When I am lecturing about music industry careers, students usually ask me two questions: "Are there jobs in the music and recording industry?" *and* "How do I go about locating and landing those jobs?" This book will answer those questions and also provide you with an introduction to the career development tools, workshop exercises, and job search strategies that will increase your chances of success in this highly competitive field.

What kinds of opportunities are out there? What kind of research skills will you need to uncover those opportunities? And how do you get plugged into specific job opportunities and develop a network where you can find out about job leads as they come up?

In the music and recording industry—or MRI, as I like to refer to it—what kinds of opportunities might there be? First and foremost, you should assess whether you are getting into the industry because you love music, you want to get rich, or because you hope to develop a long-lasting career.

In the following chapters of *How to Get a Job in the Music and Recording Industry*, we'll get down to an in-depth look at the recording studio business. That's the business that I've been involved in for more than twenty years. The recording industry provides a microcosm of the entertainment industry as a whole. Certain rules and regulations apply career-wise, and a lot of those rules you will find apply to other career paths, be they at a record label, a management company, an Internet music start-up, a booking agency, or a tour company. So, dissecting the career path in one segment of the industry will help you to see what makes up a career ladder, as well as what kind and depth of information you will need to discover with respect to your own particular field of interest.

You'll find out how to develop a marketable skill set and skills inventory. Because if you haven't identified what makes you special or valuable to an employer, chances are when you send in a resume or go for an interview, you won't communicate a clear message that positions you to win that job.

This book will help teach you to differentiate yourself in the job market so that a person hiring will see that you are a person who has something special to offer them.

You will learn about internships, and then we'll get into what it takes to conduct a job search. Some of you may be actively looking for a job now. Others may be just beginning to think about what kind of career opportunities exist. Either way, you will have a much better perspective on how to succeed after you read and work through the text and workshops in this book.

Discover what kind of tools you need for your job search. It may surprise you that most people already have a majority of them. We're going to talk about goal-setting for career development. Your goal is to get a job, but that sometimes seems like a distant objective. So we're going to break that down into smaller tasks for you, so you can make the first milestone on your journey to finding and keeping your dream job. Small steps will lead to your eventual goal, which is landing a great job.

Then we'll tackle the oft-dreaded resume. This is the task that creates the most hangdog looks from students I teach and many job seekers. I have often heard, "I don't know how to write a resume. Why do I have to have one? I just want to push faders, play my axe, and listen to great music all night."

Well, I'm here to give you the news: You *must* have a strong resume. I keep my resume current even though I own my own company. It's a critical tool you will need throughout your career, whatever field you're in.

You probably are wondering, how do you get your resume into the preferred pile of contenders and not the rejection pile? You will learn how to build a resume that clearly communicates your special skills and worth to future employers, thereby separating yourself from other job seekers.

In addition to a well-crafted resume, you will need to do some research on the jobs that interest you. How do you get started on your job search? Have you established some short-term goals, and are your long-term goals in mind?

Soon you are ready to go out and start working. What do you do? What's the first step? Do you pick up a phone? Do you read the help wanted listings? Do you purchase a subscription to *Billboard* magazine? This book provides a step-by-step approach to succeeding in your job search, and will increase your odds of landing a position in the music and recording industry.

In addition to a career as a recording engineer or record producer, we'll consider alternate careers. A host of opportunities exist in a number of rapidly expanding fields such as the computer gaming industry, the Internet, new forms of broadcasting, or other affiliated fields where sound is becoming increasingly important. Many of these jobs pay significantly higher salaries than an entry-level position in a recording studio or record label.

Finally, we'll look at the view from the top as we talk with four professionals who share their experiences on making it in this competitive business. What led to their first break? What skills and attributes do they identify as crucial as you start your new career? What's the best strategy to get a foot in the door today? Read on and you will prepare yourself for a career in one of the most exciting industries there is. ⊙

part one

Today's Job Market: *The Big Picture*

Music and Recording Industry Job Realities

When I meet students and people looking to get into the music and recording industry, quite a few share a common buzzword—*passion*. They talk about their love of music and also how much music or art means to them. However, no matter how great your passion for the music business, an accurate understanding of the job realities is necessary before you plunge into developing a career in this field.

Job Supply and Demand

The reality of the music and recording industry is like all industries: it adheres to the law of job supply and demand, a basic rule of all economic systems. When it comes to jobs and opportunities, the supply of MRI jobs falls well below the demand of those wishing to enter the industry. This causes a situation that makes every job precious, even those internships that don't pay one cent. It also means that in order to better your chances for success, you have to take advantage of every single ethical opportunity to better your skills and status in the industry.

When I was managing a recording studio, we would receive an average of four to five resumes a week. Half of those job seekers would follow up with a phone call. Some would say, "I'd love to just stop by, meet you, see the room, see the studio." Others would boldly state, "I'll do anything to get started, from scrubbing the bathroom to running for lunches."

When there are more people willing to work for no pay, it makes it harder to get paid. That's the first reality you'll discover about entry-level positions in the MRI.

The second reality is that when it comes to succeeding as a recording artist, the vast majority of recordings fail to break even for their record label. A well-known manager and label president shared a staggering statistic quoted in *Billboard:* Of the approximately 32,000 records released each year, only 189 sell at least 250,000 copies, which is considered the "break-even" point for major labels.

Making a hit record is a bit like the lottery. Only a little over one half of one percent of people break even. The other 99.5 percent fail to do so. Don't be discouraged by this statistic.

Instead, understand that although it can be done, it's a long shot to hit it big as a recording artist. That's why I encourage you to look at careers not only as a recording artist or record producer, but at the cornucopia of other jobs in the MRI industry. Don't lock yourself into one career path.

Playing for a Team

Talent, perseverance, and people skills are givens to making it in the business. A colleague who worked as a tech at George Lucas's renowned Skywalker Sound once said, "Fifty-one percent of my job is getting along with my coworkers, and 49 percent of my job is knowing how to keep all of our technology running." Her statement has stayed with me over the years as one of the most important pieces of information I could share with you.

To make it in the music and recording industry, you've got to be able to work in a group environment. If you would rather work alone, be your own boss, compose on your own, perform on your own, then perhaps you shouldn't be working in a studio, or for a record label or management company. Why? Because you've got to be able to get along with people around you. Don't panic now if "people skills" don't appear to be among your strongest talents—you can develop them. Basically it's just a matter of wanting to play on a winning team.

Climbing to the Top

Perseverance is obviously a big asset. Depending on the opportunity, there may be from 25 to 250 or more people knocking on the door for every MRI job opening. You've got to be willing to persevere. Otherwise you're going to run out of gas in your quest.

Just about everybody starts out at the bottom in this business, even today's top dogs. I encourage you to read one of the books penned by a top record label executive. One such book is *Follow the Music* by Jac Holzman, the founder of Elektra Records. (All books referenced can be found in the Resource section at the back of this book.) Seeing that just about every top executive started out as a mail clerk or assistant will help you strengthen your resolve to climb the mountain ahead with respect to your MRI career.

The benefit of starting out at the bottom of the company's organizational chart is that you meet a lot of people on the way up, you see how a company works, and you learn about every function in an organization. It's very helpful to learn about what parts work efficiently as well as what parts may not run smoothly, and more importantly, the reason why.

Competition is central to the industry. There's always new blood coming in—

new bands, new songwriters, new musicians, new Artist & Repertoire (A&R) staffers. It's the nature of the game. You've got to have a bit of a competitive streak in you to make it in this business.

Radio and television both use a formal rating system. That's the way the entertainment industry works. The anecdote that a recording artist is "only as good as the sales of their last record" is true in an economic sense. Competition is always going to be there so you have to have the drive—what's often referred to as the "fire in the belly"—to stick with your dream and push yourself to make it. Few, if any, things will come easy to you as you journey along your career path in the MRI. You will be earning your stripes every step of the way.

Hobby or Career?

Are you pursuing a hobby or a career? Why is it important to know the difference? This is an issue that sometimes trips people up as they look to make a career in the music and recording industry. Many come to the industry because of their love of music. But the reality is, you've got to have bankable skills to deliver, or you're not going to be gainfully employed or grow your career. Many people have sacrificed years of their life because they felt they wanted to be "near the music."

A hobby is the pursuit of a field for personal enjoyment. I'm a hobby guitar player today, and I play my guitar once or twice a month. I used to be a professional guitarist, and I was paid well for my skills.

A career is your vocation, the daily occupation in which you *must* excel. Either a hobby or a career can be rewarding; however, you have to decide which one of these roads you're on.

If you plan to make a career in the MRI, you've got to be serious about developing your job search strategies, building your skill set, and researching what competition you'll face in specific entry-level job areas. Discover what your earning prospects are.

It's okay to switch from hobby to career. But make sure you have the required commitment, as the road will be difficult and you will need to stay focused on achieving your goals.

WORKSHOP 1:
Create Your Own Career Book

Start by purchasing a sturdy three-ring binder. I recommend a two-and-a-half- or three-inch model. In front of the first tab divider, you should include two one-year calendars, one for the current year and a second for the following year. This will come in handy to mark important events, deadlines, and tasks for which you have set a completion date.

Then create the following sections in your career book using sheet dividers with ID tabs.

Correspondence. Keep letters to and from the various persons and companies you will encounter in your career development.

Clippings. Every time you come across an article that interests you, especially those that identify specific companies, photocopy it or clip it and add it to your career binder.

Events. Record information on industry conferences, conventions, charity events, or any other type of function that may provide you with the chance to meet and learn from others.

Jobs. Compile job descriptions, help wanted listings, references to specific positions, or internship opportunities.

Lectures. Include notes, handouts, and other classroom or lecture materials that relate to your MRI career journey.

My Journal. You are embarking on a process of career development that includes a component of self-discovery and personal evaluation. Workshop 2 will give you a start on developing the material for this section.

My Resume. The evolution of your resume and your skills at resume development will fit in here.

Target Companies. Any time you hear or read about a new company that interests you, start a new page with the company's name and URL on it. Fill in more information as you discover it.

As you journey down your own unique career path, feel free to add new sections as you need them. Perhaps you'll start a section to record details of the job and informational interviews you have. Keep some blank sheets of lined paper in the front so that you can quickly jot down notes or details of a conversation, a reference book, or a company's contact information.

The importance of your career book will become clear as the variety and amount of information that you uncover widens. Don't be concerned at first if you have little to include in each of the sections. By the time you finish reading this book and completing the workshops, you will have plenty to add.

Keeping your career binder up to date and at hand gives you instant access to the information you develop. This can be an important time saver when you or a colleague are hunting for a specific piece of data.

The final benefit to starting your career book today is that you have now made a visible investment of your time and brainpower to get your journey started properly!

The purpose of your career book is to build a dossier or backlog of resource information that you can continually refer to. A number of my former students come back, call, or write, often three or four years after our interaction, and say, "I'm so glad I kept my career book going. I sent that guest lecturer an e-mail and she sent me back a tip on a company I am investigating. From that I landed an interview!"

The whole MRI business is interconnected. And it's important to remember where to find things and where to look for people. Your career book should have sections on careers that interest you today, clippings on companies that are expanding, notes from meetings, articles on new technology, or magazine interviews with people in the business you admire. If you are interested in a career in recording, locate a list of studios in your region, as well as facilities in New York, Los Angeles, and Nashville. Go through their Web pages, print out a few that tell you what kind of work they do, and add those to your career book.

A career book becomes a reference work to help you determine which career paths interest you and will be a good fit for you. You'll find that over the years it will become a valued resource: a shortcut to get you closer from where you are today to where you want to be tomorrow. Keep that information at your fingertips. And when the first binder is full, begin another one.

Visualization

Another very important step for your career is to visualize yourself in your target career. For instance, if your career goal is to become a professional songwriter, you have to cross that bridge and say, "I *am* a songwriter. Okay, now that I'm a songwriter, how do I get to be a *better* songwriter?" That's a critical career step.

Once you see yourself developing in this new career, it doesn't matter if you're going to work by day as a paralegal, a waitress, a grocery clerk, or a data-entry "droid." Because in your heart, you know that you are working on developing your career and that you're a songwriter. If becoming a songwriter is your MRI career goal, rename your career book, "Songwriter Career Book." Your career book is a key resource you construct over time to help you reach your career destination.

Making Connections to Grow Your Career

The MRI industry is forever evolving, and currently it is morphing itself via the Internet. Within five years, the means that artists use to promote themselves, to sell records (or downloads), and appear live will all be changed by the explosion of the information revolution. To keep up with the changes, you've got to commit yourself to continuous learning. It's interesting because in the years that I've been teaching a MRI career class, the students who are thinking about making a career change have become more skewed towards people thirty to forty-five years of age.

It is vitally important that you become well read on the industry and that you talk to people who are working in the business. If you find ways to meet people that are doing what you want to do and ask them intelligent questions, you will most likely discover your path to get into the business. That is the surest way to be aware of the changing trends that affect our business.

As an example, in the Northern California region there's a songwriting organization, Northern California Songwriters Association (NCSA). They host an outstanding annual fall symposium. You should attend the symposium if you live in the region and want to make it as a songwriter. You should be networking with other songwriters. You've got to be talking to those publishers who are in attendance at the NCSA fall symposium. That's your Super Bowl. You have to be there. You've got to commit yourself to lifelong learning and getting involved with others doing what you aspire to do.

Here's another example for those of you aspiring to be record producers. At the Audio Engineering Society (AES) Convention in the fall, and the National Association of Music Merchandisers (NAMM) conventions in winter and summer, there are producer's forums that are open to the public for a small admission fee cohosted by the Recording Academy. You can listen to some of the most successful producers in the business talk about what it takes to make it is as a producer. Top producers talk for two hours about what they do, how they got their breaks, and what they recommend for an up-and-coming producer of the future. How can you miss that if you want to be the next Don Was or Babyface? You've got to find opportunities to learn and network such as these.

If you can't get to an event, find out if there is a tape or transcript, or whether it was broadcast on the Internet. This information is out there. The people who have presented and appeared at the event are usually happy to talk to you in the right setting, and share the information and ideas and experience that they have. You've got to always be looking for opportunities to soak up more information. Become an information "sponge." Fill your career book with clippings, notes, and information on careers and companies that pique your interest and spark your imagination.

Obviously, you've got to learn and practice your craft too. You've got to keep engineering or writing songs, you've got to keep booking bands, whatever avocation you aspire to. But focus part of your energy on getting near people that are doing what you want to do at the highest level possible. Because that's the fastest way to learn about the "do's and don'ts" and the "ins and outs" of our business. There is no substitute for exposure to working professionals. ⊙

Why Geography Matters

This is your MRI geography lesson. On the map below are the most important cities in the United States for the MRI: New York, Nashville, and Los Angeles.

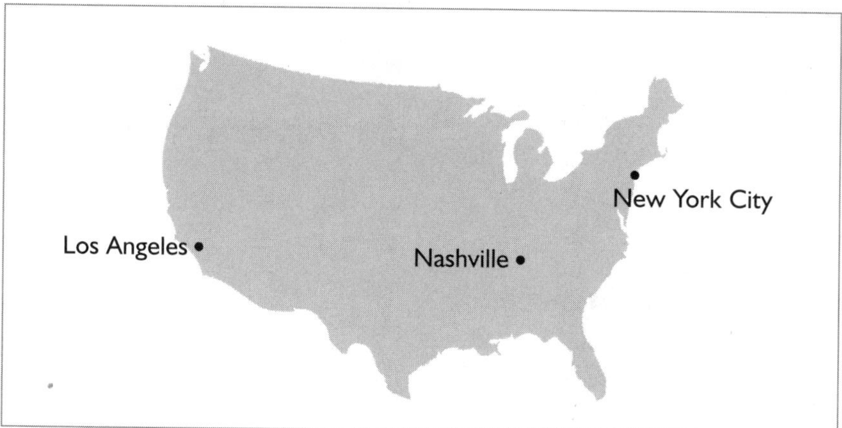

For the record business in North America, these cities represent the top of the mountain. If you aspire to make it to the top, at some point you're going to go to one of these three cities. That's where it happens for the record business. So if you're recording, if you're a songwriter, an engineer/producer, or if you're going to work with a label, sooner or later you will be living or working in one of these three regions.

Don't despair if you aren't living now in one of the major cities. If you live in Seattle, Chicago, San Francisco, Atlanta, Miami, Boston, St. Louis, Denver, or another metropolitan area, you can develop an excellent skill set. You can work at an Indie label or with promotion companies, learn how to make a great-sounding recording, and build up your skills without having to be in such a big shark-tank where there is such intense competition that you need buckets of ambition and drive to succeed.

Rather than jumping feet-first into one of the top three music markets, it's an excellent strategy to work in a smaller market to really learn the basics of how the industry works. It may be helpful to work with a concert promoter, a booking agency, or other related firm in your area of interest. One day you will feel that you may have outgrown your situation and that you're ready to take the next step in your career development.

When my former students tell me they are ready to make their move to the big markets, I suggest they visit first. I tell them to take two weeks off from their current job, travel to one of the major markets, and rent a room or stay with a friend to do some networking and some interviewing. You need to make sure that you're ready to go on to the next level. Moving to one of the top markets is expensive, and it's emotionally intense. Check it out before you pull up your stakes and jump in. You have to have your eyes open before you take the plunge. Prepare yourself to succeed when you make your move to one of these three regions. Those are the practicalities of MRI geography. ⊙

What Kinds of Jobs Are There in the MRI?

When I first started teaching a class on careers in the MRI, people asked, "Well, what jobs are there besides songwriter, musician, or recording engineer?" Look carefully anywhere that music or sound is needed, and you'll discover dozens of jobs to investigate. The list at the end of this chapter reveals a range of jobs. Affiliated music and sound careers abound in the film, theater, and educational arenas. Education is an often-overlooked career path, but it's essential, because if no one is learning how to make music, there won't be any music—or at least a whole lot less of it.

Television and radio, computer hardware and software, video games, theme parks. At Disney, rather than calling their audio staff "engineers," they call them "imagineers." I like that terminology. Think of all the sounds there are at a theme park such as a Disney or Universal Studios location. Imagineers not only create the sounds, but they also design the playback systems and keep the sound running around the clock.

Telecommunicators, recording equipment, the latest sound equipment, recorders, compressors, reverbs, amplifiers, mixing boards, and microphones. Someone has to imagine, design, and build them all. Perhaps you're interested in music publishing or journalism? Or what about working at a record company, as it will have all the positions of any other going business, from mail clerk to president. You will soon read about careers in recording studios in much greater detail.

Do you know what a "Foley artist" does? A Foley artist recreates the background sounds in feature movies, such as an *Indiana Jones* epic. When the actors are running through the jungle, the sound of the actors running wasn't recorded while they were filming. All of those sounds you hear of the hyenas, the tropical birds, the footsteps, and the waterfall were all created afterward in a sound studio. The Foley artist or artists create all the human-generated sounds such as footsteps, body hits, punches, doors being opened and closed, and even the sounds of bedclothes or curtains rustling in a breeze. It's a fascinating field. And the artists who do the work are in great demand.

If you go see a low-budget movie, then perhaps most of the Foley and sound effects are coming out of a sampling keyboard or computer that plays back sounds from a digital sound effects library. But when you see a movie by George Lucas, Stephen Spielberg, James Cameron, or other mainstream

Hollywood directors, Foley artists have added the Foley work the old-fashioned way. If you listen very carefully to both types of films, you will hear that the old-fashioned way sounds most realistic.

For the sound of the T-Rex in the film *Jurassic Park*, a team of sound designers at Skywalker Sound spent days developing that one growl to make it believable. After all, who really knows what a T-Rex growl sounds like? But the sound they imagined, and then created, has a strong impact.

Music editor, sound editor, singer, songwriter, personal manager, publicist, music video director, record producer, project manager. For example, a project manager plays a huge role for a software company like Electronic Arts or Sega. These firms have twenty, thirty, or more project managers on staff, managing teams and developing new games. On each team, there are programmers, writers, consultants, digital artists, cinematographers, sound editors, and budget analysts. A complex interactive video game has to come together in a precise manner. The project manager is the person responsible for making sure it's all rolling forward and will make the target dates.

Music educator, music librarian, copyist. What does a copyist do? They copy music. Computers, using notation software, generate more and more music scores. But copyists can also arrange music used by bands, symphonies, or orchestras for film scores, television commercials, music dates, and the like.

Newcomers to the music and recording industry have often been attracted to the field by the glamour of a particular job or artistic pursuit. There are thousands of successful recording artists, but for each one, there are at least fifty support people behind them, many in high-paying, exciting careers. They may not share the spotlight on stage, but they have very rewarding careers in the music and recording industry.

In the resource section at the end of the book is a listing for a book that provides an overview of many different jobs that relate to our industry, *Career Opportunities in the Music Industry*, by Shelly Field. Find a copy and look at it to see the diversity of MRI jobs. Also, if you are enrolled in a college or vocational program your school may have a career day where local professionals visit and talk about what they do everyday in their jobs.

Getting to know about the variety of jobs and what kinds of skills and aptitude are required for each is one of the most important activities you can undertake. How can you find out if you are well-suited for a job if you don't know what it takes to do it well?

After reviewing some of the general fields listed below, as well as a few specific jobs, start your own list today of the jobs that most intrigue you.

Keep your list handy in your career book. (You *have* started your career book, haven't you?)

Hopefully, the list below will get you thinking about the dozens of jobs that you may never have known about in our industry.

On the right-hand side of the chart are career fields, and on the left-hand side, selected job titles. You could add another dozen if you thought about it and started reading up on what's happening today in the music and recording biz.

MUSIC AND RECORDING INDUSTRY JOBS

Selected job titles

Recording Studio Manager
Recording Studio Scheduler
Sales or Marketing Department
Maintenance Engineer *(repair)*
Foley Artist
ADR Mixer
Sound Designer
Composer
Disc Jockey
Location Recordist
Sound Editor
Software Designer
Compressionist
Music Editor
Singer
Songwriter
Personal Manager
Business Manager
Music Attorney
Publicist
Instrumentalist *(live or studio)*
Arranger
Copyist
Music Librarian
Recording Engineer
Producer/Project Manager
Program Director
Research and Development Engineer
Editor/Writer *(journalism and publishing)*
Music Educator

General fields relying on sound and music skills

record companies *(all functions)*
recording studio
film music/soundtracks
theater music
music education
television production
radio
computer hardware *(sound)*
computer software *(music and sound)*
video games
theme parks
telecommunications
recording equipment
live sound reinforcement
music journalism
music publishing

These are only a handful of jobs and fields that need talented newcomers to jump on and help make a difference. By the time you are reading this, there will be many new job titles created as our industry continues to evolve and change in the face of new technologies. Don't limit your view to one or two career paths. Do some serious investigation before you settle on any one route. ⦿

chapter 4

Gizmos, People, and Gender

It's a fact. Most people prefer to work with either technology or people. Now is an appropriate time for you to ascertain whether you are primarily a "people person" or what I call a "gizmologist," a gizmo and technology person.

How can you do that? Consider this hypothetical question. Suppose you're working as an intern at a record label in L.A. You have the opportunity to help a label producer set up the new demo studio or to give the tour to a group of businessmen to show them how the label is structured. Which do you prefer?

The answer to that question may lead you to evaluate—*do I like working with technology or do I prefer working with people?* It's important to know your preference. You've got to be able to do both today, to some degree. You've got to be familiar with computers and the Internet. You really can't start a career in the entertainment industry today without knowledge in these areas. Regardless of your proclivity for technology or working with people, your career in the music and recording industry will require you to become proficient at interpersonal skills, listening, talking, and networking. Even the most hardcore programmer will need to have a network of colleagues who know them and support their career development. Don't fall into the trap of believing that your technology chops alone will get you to the top. Without a reasonable complement of interpersonal and networking skills, tech skills alone won't lead anywhere in the MRI.

If you wake up at night thinking about ways to wire your home studio together to reduce the noise floor, you're likely a gizmo person. If so, you have good career opportunities ahead, because it's essential that there be gizmologists to keep the music world wired and working. Technology is a core component of recording, producing, and, now, merchandising music via the Internet.

Visualize a singer with a guitar playing a song to a roomful of people, with no microphone, no PA, no electronics. The minute that singer has to perform for a larger audience, you need technology. You've got to have mics, cable, amps, TV monitors, and a person to run them.

The "people" side of the business is equally important. Companies must set goals and objectives, develop the means to accomplish those goals, manage team building, finance, sales, promotion, and human resources, and tackle long-term planning. Those tasks are people related. Hence, business-types provide the structure needed to make a record label, recording studio, or other music-related business a success.

That's why you should consider which you prefer, people or gizmos, so you can focus your career research in an area that suits you. Interestingly, the people who make it to the very top of the industry are generalists, meaning that they have experience in both areas. They may be stronger in one or the other, but they are conversant in both.

So, you'll find that the top person in most big organizations is adept at delegating and managing, and is a good judge of people. He or she has the ability to say, "Here's a person, and this is what motivates them and how they can contribute to our company's effort." These kinds of leaders usually have a good grasp of technology—not only of where things are today, but where they're headed in the future. Lastly, top leaders share one other common trait: an unquenchable desire to succeed.

Equal Opportunity for All?

Males have traditionally dominated the music and recording industry. Historically, 90 percent of the people working in recording studios, concert production, and most technical roles were male, and few women were found behind the mixing console. That has changed over the last ten years. In terms of the recording industry, there are now opportunities for women to work as engineers, producers, A&R execs, technicians, label presidents, and any position that men have traditionally held. Although the number of women working at record labels has been high historically, it's only recently that women are common in the top ranks.

A lot of ancillary fields, such as live sound, concert production, staging, cartage, and rigging, are still dominated by men today. A woman aspiring to a career in the MRI must be aware that there are a lot of people who have been in the industry for many years who possess extremely chauvinistic attitudes. A woman should be mentally prepared for that. She has to have faith in herself, and know what strengths she has and how she can utilize them. She has to conscientiously work to say and act upon what she believes in. The fix is to have the skills and ambition to do the job well, and you will move ahead on your career path. Women such as Madonna, Sylvia Rhone, Sarah McLachlan, Queen Latifah, Sheryl Crow, Melissa Etheridge, Reba McEntire, Alanis Morissette, Ani DiFranco, and many others are influencing our industry, and you can do it too. ⊙

Career Ladders in the Recording Industry: *The Technical Career Track*

Get ready to dive into the staff structure of a world-class recording studio for an in-depth look at each rung of the music recording career ladder. Similar career ladders exist in the record company, management, booking and tour agencies, performing rights societies, and other career paths. If you are interested in becoming a recording engineer, producer, studio owner, manager, or scheduler, here's the scoop on those jobs. For readers interested in other career paths, reading these chapters carefully will give a good idea of the hierarchy that exists in every music and recording industry business sector.

We talked earlier about the "music business." There's the *music*, and then there's the *business*. In the recording studio business, there is the art and craft of recording—that is, what goes on in the actual recording session, plus the management of the studio business. Thus, there are two career tracks. The chart on this page shows the Technical Career Track in the recording studio.

TECHNICAL CAREER TRACK—RECORDING STUDIO

Gofer

Tape Copyist

Assistant Engineer

Studio Maintenance Engineer

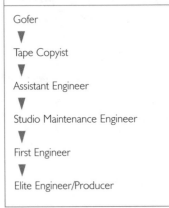

First Engineer

Elite Engineer/Producer

As a point of reference, the charts and data in this chapter are indicative of a multiroom commercial recording facility in a major market. The first three rungs on the ladder may have different names and duties, depending on the nature of the work being done at a particular studio. The one common aspect of all three, however, is that they are learning stops on the path to a successful career in the recording studio business.

Let's look at the first job on the technical track, and find out just what a **Gofer** does. Gofers (also known as studio assistants) absorb everything that goes on at a studio and learn how important all the little details are in making a studio operation run smoothly. They "go for" coffee, cigarettes, lunches, tequila... whatever the studio or artist needs at that moment. What if the bass player gets a flat tire in the parking lot? A gofer helps change the flat. Go for this, go for that, help with this, deal with that. Gofers get to see just about every side of the daily operation of a recording studio and the front lines of the business.

If you're competent as a gofer, you will be promoted to be a **Tape Copyist**. What does this job entail? You make copies in the "Xerox room" of the recording studio. "I've got this tape, I need twenty copies." "I've got this song, I need five CDs." "I've got this 78 rpm recording, I need a copy." "I've got a ZIP disk with MP3 files on it and need to post it to the FTP page on my label's Web site." A tape copyist starts to learn about recording technology in a situation that is less demanding than a client-attended recording session. As tape becomes less prevalent in the recording studio environment, being replaced by hard disks and recordable optical media, the job title may be reduced simply to "copyist" or "dubber."

This position and function is critical to learning many of the basic skills that an engineer will draw on throughout their career. If you can't align a tape for proper playback and then copy it, you can forget about actually participating in a recording session. You're never going to get that far. So rather than looking at the tape copyist position as drudgery, it should be viewed as an excellent opportunity to learn about the many formats and technologies that an engineer and a studio must be familiar with today.

Making a perfect copy is the acid test. You've got to know every format. You've got to know every alignment, and over time become familiar with every record and playback procedure in the studio. And while you are working as a tape copyist, you will also develop people skills with clients. A client will call and say, "I've got to have this copy by two o'clock." When the tape arrives, it turns out to be in an arcane format. That will force you to stretch and learn and grow your skill set to get that particular job done and satisfy your client.

Tape copyist is a very important job, not only because the studio needs to provide the service, but because it's a fantastic way to learn and practice basic recording skills in a situation that is much less pressure-packed than a recording session. And it's one whose importance is often overlooked.

In fact, I've been involved in situations where gofers were offered a promotion to tape copyist and they answered, "No, I won't do it because I want to go work in the recording studio." Guess what happened to most of those people? They're gone. If you're reasonably adept as a tape copyist, you will get your opportunity to move up and become an assistant engineer.

The job title **Assistant Engineer** perfectly describes the job function. Assistants (or seconds, as they are also known) set up the recording studio for a session, handle the cables properly, place microphones once they have learned how to do that task, and assist the first engineer throughout the session. An assistant engineer accelerates his/her learning process after a successful stint as a gofer and tape copyist by assisting and observing the senior engineering staff during recording sessions every day.

Another important function an assistant performs is session documentation. A colleague of mine has recently been working with members of the group Earth, Wind & Fire. He said that they're recording tracks for a new album. "We've already recorded 100 rolls of two-inch, 24-track tape of new material." All those tapes have to be fully documented and logged. Each master reel's contents must be written up, then put into a computer. That's one of the assistant's critically important responsibilities. If it's not done properly, how will the producer, engineer, or artist locate the material they need among the hundreds of takes and thousands of tracks when they continue the project?

As an assistant engineer you're going to use a computer daily. Get comfortable with computers because it is an essential tool for documenting and managing information in the recording studio.

When you're working as an assistant engineer, you are exposed to clients more fully. You also work with the senior technical staff to develop a better understanding of how an engineer functions productively in a commercial studio, and in the process will help to generate revenue and profits.

Occasionally, a technically adept assistant engineer may consider moving into studio maintenance after a stint as an assistant engineer. Today's **Studio Maintenance Engineer** is truly a jack-of-all-trades. Ten years ago, the emphasis in maintenance was on electrical and mechanical aptitude. Digital recording still meant that magnetic tape was rolling. Today, a maintenance engineer must be as equally comfortable eliminating a software glitch as he is in tweaking a vintage analog 2-track tape recorder or a Fairchild tube limiter. Talented maintenance engineers are seldom out of work for very long. After all, if you were a studio owner with a multimillion-dollar investment, and your revenue earning was based on fully functioning studios, wouldn't you keep the best maintenance personnel available on staff?

If you prove to have good technical aptitude as an assistant engineer and your boss finds out that you know how to "fix things," you may be groomed for a tech or maintenance gig. Perhaps as a kid growing up you built radio-controlled model cars, or you actually learned how to repair your own car or motorcycle. If the studio manager finds out about those skills, you could be in for a promotion before you know it. Studio maintenance is an area that offers financial security like few other jobs in the recording industry. A competent studio maintenance engineer knows how to keep everything running in a modern studio, keep maintenance logs, work with management, and develop a basic maintenance budget. With these skills you'll seldom experience unemployment. You will be able to go to New York, Los Angeles, or Nashville and start at $40,000–$50,000 a year. It'll go up from there if you are adept at keeping the studio equipment running well.

Of course, today's maintenance engineer also has to know a good deal about computers. They must understand tapes and tape transports, both analog and digital. A solid knowledge of digital audio and Society of Motion Picture and Television Engineers (SMPTE) time code is required. You take the skills you've developed in these areas and use it. A studio maintenance person may begin their career development as an assistant maintenance engineer or a night maintenance engineer for a few years to hone their skills. Then they may move to another studio and be top dog in maintenance. Such a career can be very rewarding, not only financially, but also in knowing that you are responsible for keeping the studio and its clients "on the air."

Most engineers don't take the maintenance path because there are fewer openings, and frankly, to many it's not as appealing as making the move from assistant to **First Engineer**. This move usually happens when something special occurs, such as working with a hit artist. That may be what it takes to break out. Or a staff first engineer may leave to go independent, and you are the next logical person to assume the role of staff first engineer.

Or, if you've stuck around long enough, you've earned the respect of senior staff so that the first engineers are thinking, "I don't want to do that session tonight. It doesn't start until nine o'clock. Laura could handle it." And just like that, you are "firsting" a paying session on your own and putting the skills to work that you have developed since you started as a gofer some time back.

After I "graduated" from Bayshore Studios, my 8-track studio, to Music Annex, which was a multiroom, 24-track facility, one day a popular first engineer got double booked. So he said, "Keith, go do that session in Studio A." My hesitant reply was, "I've n-n-n-never worked in Studio A with a 24-track machine and Neve board before." His response was, "Ah, it's no problem, you can do it."

The session was with a well-known gospel artist, and she brought a three-year-old girl for a duet with no advance notice! So I set up a Neumann U-67 microphone and this little girl was in the room seated at the grand piano with the artist. I could barely hear the toddler when she was singing along because her voice output in the room was so low. My debut as a "first engineer" quickly turned into a nightmare session.

Somehow, I barely got the performance on tape. How was my debut as a first engineer? A disaster, and the track was unusable. So, needless to say, the next session I helmed, I was *ready*. I was empowered, totally prepared, everything was set up ahead of time, and the session went very well. It became *fun*. I really learned from being thrown into the fire on the previous date. I also learned that it is okay to quickly point out if something is not going well at the outset of the session. The artist or producer may be a bit miffed, but not anywhere near as angry as if a great performance in the studio didn't make it to tape because you, in your role as first engineer, didn't identify a problem early in the session.

The first engineer's role is basically to get the performance on tape, whatever that takes. They have to interface with the artist. They're part shrink, part den mother, and sometimes part slave-driver. They must know when to say to the artist, "That's still not right, you can get that more in tune." A first engineer has to walk a fine line between technology and psychology to get the best performance possible on tape, and not to push the artist too far. Sometimes that second take really *was* the best one. By going for the perfect take over and over, sometimes you may actually be regressing and not improving the track. The first engineer has technical as well as a bit of artistic responsibility to ensure that the session is flowing smoothly and that the artist's performance is being faithfully captured.

As a "first," your opinion now will count in every aspect of the studio's business. You'll be asked to review and recommend equipment for purchase, take junior members of the staff under your wing for guidance and shaping, assist in selling key artists and producers on using your studio for projects, and have a voice in the long-term planning and direction of the studio at which you work.

You'll also be exposed to a wide range of artists, producers, and talented individuals, all of which will broaden your palette of experience and engineering expertise. Your voice and your opinion will be critical to the success of the recording projects you work on as you build confidence, respect, and camaraderie with the staff and clients you interact with.

Eventually, if you're a really outstanding engineer, you may have the opportunity to evolve into an **Elite Engineer/Producer**. Examples include Brendan O'Brien, Bob Clearmountain, Al Schmitt, Butch Vig, Sylvia Massy, Trevor Horn, Jimmy Jam and Terry Lewis, Phil Ramone, Tony Brown, and Sir George Martin.

Two things differentiate the elite class of engineer/producer from an outstanding first engineer. One is their body of work, and specifically what type of success they have enjoyed in terms of units sold for the records done. The second is what you earn, which can be ten to one hundred times more than a first engineer, because at this stage of your career you are in demand. Elite engineer/producers may even command a percentage of an album's earnings if they are really hot. You still may perform many of the same tasks you did when you were an established first. Now, however, you've got the "golden touch." The other skill that an elite engineer/producer develops is the ability to handle the politics and the recording budgets between the artist, their management, and the record label—which is an entirely different skill set in addition to engineering and producing a great record.

Studio Salaries

What do the gofers earn? Tape copyists? And what does an assistant engineer get paid? Here's the scoop.

TECHNICAL CAREER TRACK—RECORDING STUDIO

	Salary Range
Gofer	Free–$8/hour
Tape Copyist	Free–$12/hour
Assistant Engineer	Free–$15/hour
Studio Maintenance	$10–30/hour
First Engineer	$15–35/hour
Elite Engineer/Producer	$50/hour to "the sky's the limit"

I'm sure you've noticed that the three jobs at the start of this career have a common element—a salary range varying from *free* to a modest hourly wage. Every reputable studio has a steady stream of persons calling, writing, and visiting who will do anything to "get into the business." This never-ending parade of people is willing to sweep the floor, run errands, and scrub the dishes for free. This means that if you want to gain an entry-level position in the recording studio business, you have to be willing to work and learn for little or no money until you can prove your worth.

The more knowledge and savvy you can demonstrate, the faster the opportunities will open up for you. Ultimately, every studio manager or owner has to view each employee's contributions to the success of the business in economic terms—"*what work did you perform or what problems did you solve for me today?*"

This leads to the question of how one supports oneself and pays for the basic cost of living if you are working for free?

One option is to save up a nest egg and take on the job with a finite time frame, for instance, enough to work for six months at entry level. If you determine that you can't afford to work for free in a studio forty hours a week, perhaps you can work part time, nights, or weekends and hold down a paying job (the inevitable "day gig") so that you are able to meet your basic living expenses.

As you move up the technical career track to studio maintenance, what will you earn? $10 to $30 an hour. What does $30 an hour equal as an annual salary? Approximately $58,000 a year (before taxes). The salary ranges referenced in this book will vary a bit from region to region. In an area with a higher cost of living, or where there is more competition for good staff, they will be a bit higher. In a smaller market, they will tend to be a bit lower.

A person in the **First Engineer** position makes $15 to $35 an hour, with the potential to even do a little better at the upper end of the experience and competency scale.

A first engineer is likely to have variations in earning if they are paid on the basis of how many sessions they engineer. In a slower month, they may earn $2,000. However, with some overtime and weekend sessions—("The masters are due at the label in five days, we have to work extra hours to finish the mix!")—a busy first may log as many as two hundred billable hours, or close to fifty billable hours a week! In that month, they might earn as much as $6,000–$7,000. That's why I have averaged the hourly earning number, in order to reflect an annual basis.

If success and a bit of luck come your way, you may make the jump into the rarefied atmosphere of the **Elite Engineer/Producer**. This is a well-established professional at the top of their craft who is in demand due to a solid track record of success. He or she has Grammy awards, a wall of multi-platinum hits, Oscars for best sound track or film score, and possibly Clio or Emmy awards for their advertising or television mixes. In the music arena, it's the producer who is able to have their manager say, "Yeah, we'll mix that single for your artist." And the mixing fee for that single can be as much as a mid-five-figure sum for the very top mixers and producers with a solid string of chart-topping credentials.

There are a handful of these star producers. That's why I like to equate this part of the technical career track to major league baseball. How many kids play Little League? I would imagine that millions do. And how many make it to the World Series? Probably twenty or thirty on each team. So it's a long shot, but some people who started years ago as gofers do make it to the top. It's not impossible.

The elite engineer/producer performs daily in the "World Series" of the recording business. This level of success allows a person to earn very handsome fees due to the time and effort they have spent mastering their art and craft. In most cases, this is ten to twenty years or more. For someone starting out in the recording or record producing game, it's great to aspire to this, but you must temper your expectations. Realize that for every few thousand gofers, perhaps one person is going to work and struggle and learn and eventually graduate to elite producer engineer. Actually, those odds are quite a bit better than major league baseball, aren't they?

Some more examples of elite engineer/producers are Bruce Swedien, Frank Fillipetti, Butch Vig, George Massenberg, Shawn Murphy, Bruce Botnick, Rick Rubin, Bob Ludwig, Tchad Blake, and Gary Rydstrom. They each have built a very strong reputation and track record, and can now command top fees for their creative contributions to albums, film soundtracks, and other projects. ⊙

Career Ladders in the Recording Industry: *The Management Career Track*

There's a parallel track to the top of the recording studio business in the area of business management. Now we'll take an in-depth look at the career path of becoming a top studio manager or owner.

Here's the ladder for the management career track in the recording studio business.

MANAGEMENT CAREER TRACK—RECORDING STUDIO

Gofer

Receptionist

Scheduler

Studio Manager/Sales

Studio Owner

No surprise, you start as a **Gofer** (or studio assistant.) You're ordering flowers, putting toilet paper in the bathrooms, scraping burnt coffee out of the bottom of the coffee pot, running errands, and doing whatever it takes to keep the studio functioning. You will likely be doing some fun stuff, too: picking up a celebrity at the airport, making script copies for a film dialog automated dialog replacement (ADR) session, or helping set up chairs, music stands, and headphones for a large orchestral date.

The next stop on the career track is that of **Receptionist**. What do receptionists do? It's pretty much the same at any business, based on its size. Receptionists answer the phones, take messages, help with the paperwork, and keep the flow of communications going throughout the studio. They basically assist those above them on the career track with the operation of the business.

What does a **Scheduler** do? They book time. If I call up and I say "I've got a forty-member choir, and I wish to come in and record a Christmas album," and the scheduler books me into a small studio used for voice-over recording, there is going to be a problem. There is going to be a similar problem if I call and say, "I'm working on a film. I've got a 16mm answer print, and I'd like to look at it and spot some library music to go with it," and the scheduler books me into a room that has VHS and Betacam video playback but no 16mm film projection. Hence, schedulers must know quite a bit about a facility's capabilities and recording technology to properly do their job.

Where do schedulers come from? Often assistant engineers who may not have the chops, the stamina, or the determination to pay their dues and make their way to first engineer become outstanding schedulers. Because they've actually worked with tape and time code, and have set up sessions and worked directly with the gear, the staff, producers, and clients, they know exactly what goes on during a recording session.

That doesn't mean that someone can't learn how to schedule effectively without ever having done any engineering work. However, it's really helpful to know something about what's going on behind the door in the studio when you're scheduling. This knowledge will become even more critical the further you get from music recording and into sound for film, video, television, broadcast, or interactive programs and games.

By comparison, scheduling for music recording is more straightforward. When an artist records a song, the scheduler normally will have musicians and singers come into the studio to lay it down on tape. Next, the engineer will overdub additional parts and mix it, the client will approve the mixes, and then the engineer will move on to the next album project. That's the usual way music recordings are made.

As soon as you start scheduling interactive, Internet sound, film, or music video projects, there are literally dozens of variables. Is the video NTSC, SECAM, or PAL (three noncompatible video playback technologies used in different parts of the world)? What frame rate was the film or video shot at? Do you need Dolby Surround, Dolby Digital, or Dolby E? Is the talent union or non-union? Is the source footage on film, video, or hard disk? Will you need library music, and if so, what genres, tempos, and instrumentation? Do you need to do a stereo mix or a separate mix with stems? What about a foreign language version? Splits for M&E (music and effects) and so on? Whew! The only way to learn and stay conversant with the myriad details involved is to immerse oneself into the daily operations of a studio doing this kind of work.

Our industry is heading into a new era of higher resolution digital audio for consumers with Super Audio CD and DVD-Audio. There are opportunities to create a virtual sonic environment with 5.1 channel surround music recordings that will allow new levels of creativity and realism never before imagined. But in general, audio post production requires an encyclopedic knowledge of formats, technologies, and trends in broadcast production and delivery technologies. Put simply, there are more "gotcha's" in post production than in music recording.

The next step on the career ladder is the **Studio Manager/Sales** position. This person acts as the right hand of the studio owner. He or she assigns tasks, helps navigate the course for the business, and often leads the staff. The studio manager will usually handle negotiations regarding lengthy bookings, any variation in studio rates, as well as personnel issues. It is their responsibility to work in tandem with the owner to see that the studio is showing a profit, so they need to be comfortable with budgets and basic accounting.

The studio manager is in charge of the day-to-day operation and the selling of studio time. When a regular client calls to book time, they usually speak with the scheduler. If a prospective client calls up and says, "Hey, I heard about your studio from another producer. I'm looking for a place to do a new album next year and I want to know more about your facility," that call will be routed to the studio manager. The studio will invite them for a tour, play some tracks for them, and may introduce them to one of the engineers who calls that studio home. They will build rapport and foster the belief that this is the right place for that specific project. It's a challenging job. There is never a dull moment when you are in charge of a commercial studio operation.

And then there is the **Studio Owner**. What does a studio owner do today? He or she manages a team of very creative (and sometimes zany or temperamental) professionals, ruminates on the nature of the next swing of the technology pendulum, constantly reviews financial profitability and performance data, and goes down to the studio at 3 a.m. when the studio's alarm has gone off! Those are just a few of the challenges that await the person who aspires to own a successful commercial facility.

When I left Music Annex in 1995, I had made one career decision for myself. After owning my own commercial studio for four years and working at another very successful facility for almost twelve years, I wasn't ever going to start a business where I had to spend more money every month buying, leasing, and maintaining equipment than I could pay myself. You see, owning a commercial recording studio means keeping up with the latest technology investments. Commercial studio ownership is not a career for the faint of heart. If you are to succeed, you quickly learn what it takes to keep clients satisfied and to keep a close eye on your overhead and bottom line.

As owner of a commercial recording studio, you are constantly considering what needs to be repaired, replaced, or upgraded. Will the new investment result in new revenue or simply in keeping your current clients and rates intact? There's not a day that goes by that you're not thinking about issues such as these.

One exception is if you own is a non-commercial studio. If you have your own studio (and hopefully the technology bug has not bitten you *too* severely), you can say, "Okay, I'm going to get my studio to a certain functional level. And then I will be satisfied for my needs. I can do my songwriting. I can do my demos. I can compose a sound track. I can even put out a homegrown CD." You aren't faced with adding more tracks, more vintage gear, a bigger lounge for the clients, a security guard for the parking lots, etc.

Today's savvy home studio owner has the option of knowing, "When I *am* ready to make my magnum opus album, I'm going to go to XYZ studio to do the parts that I can't do at my studio. They've got a bunch of great mikes, a concert grand piano, a boatload of the finest reverbs and signal processors—it's all there. And I'll rent the use of it for the hours or days that I need it. But I don't need to own that very expensive gear year round."

Heresy? No, just the voice of experience. Listen back to the *Sgt. Pepper's Lonely Hearts Club Band* album by the Beatles, and remind yourself that it was recorded more than thirty years ago by some very creative musicians, engineers, and producers on 4-track equipment that was stone-age in comparison to most of the home recording gear available today.

The chart below gives an indication as to what salaries might be expected on the studio management ladder.

MANAGEMENT CAREER TRACK—RECORDING STUDIO

	Salary Range
Gofer	Free–$8/hour
Receptionist	$8–$15/hour
Scheduler	$12–25/hour
Studio Manager/Sales	$20–35/hour
Studio Owner	Feast or famine—it's up to you!

If you compare the earning power of these positions to the ones on the technical career track, one thing is immediately apparent at the early stage: there are far fewer unpaid positions in the management track.

The second difference is that there is a much greater range from the low- to the high-salary range for each position. That is due to two factors. First, the size of the studio business: larger studio operations will generally be able to pay more. The second factor is location. A successful studio in one of the top markets will offer a more attractive compensation package to attract and retain top talent on their business team. Commercial studios in smaller regional markets will not be able to offer as much.

In a top market at a successful studio, a scheduler can expect to top out at around to $50,000 in annual salary, while a studio manager may earn as much as $75,000 or more managing a top multiroom Hollywood, New York, or London studio. And then we have the owner. What is his or her salary range? Whatever they can pull out of a business that demands an incredible amount of attention, financial investment, and personal commitment. Some studio owners drive Ferraris and others drive Toyotas. There is no formula other than following careful business practices to ensure that the commercial studio generates as much profit as possible in any given year.

Not Interested in a Recording Studio Career?

Not to worry. Keep these two career ladders from the recording studio in mind whether or not you envision yourself in a recording studio setting. Why? Because no matter what sector of the music or recording industry you pursue, I can assure you that there will be a very similar ladder of increasing responsibility, challenges, and rewards in the technical and business arena.

For instance, if you decide you would like to be head of A&R at a record label or program director at a top radio station, you will need to do the research necessary to map out a career ladder similar to the ones outlined in the previous chapters. Determine the specific job titles, responsibilities, and earning potential on the career track leading to your goal. Researching and understanding the nitty-gritty details of the career ladder will help you avoid investing in a career path that may never meet your expectations for creative or financial development. ⊙

part two

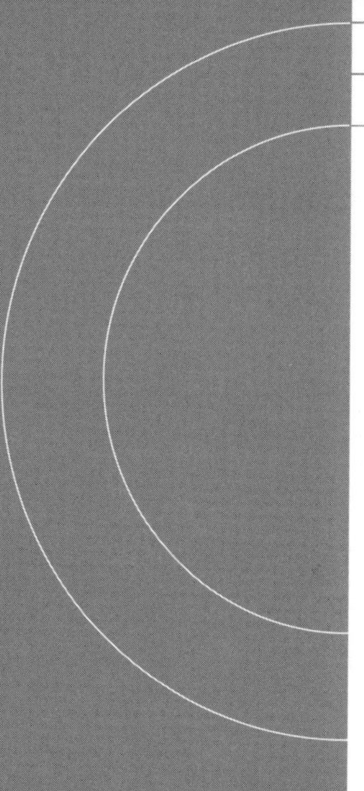

Excuse Me, What **Do** You Do?

The chapter's title is not meant to pose a facetious question. If you don't have a thorough understanding of the skills, responsibilities, hours, pay range, and future prospects for a particular job in the music and recording industry, how can you assess whether or not you have (or can develop) the skills and connections to land that job?

There are two ways to research what working professionals actually do. The first and by far the more accessible method is to read up on a particular job. Second, keep up with current trade magazines covering the segment of the industry that you wish to enter. If you aspire to be a label exec, agent, musician, or producer, then go to the library and check out a few biographies that chronicle the path that various artists or executives have taken to the top. Record producer Sir George Martin, musician Al Kooper, label executive Jac Holzman, and super agent Ian Copeland each have inked compelling biographies. Richard Buskin's *Inside Tracks* provides mini-interviews of many of the most influential record producers of the last fifty years of pop music. *Masters of Music*, by Mark Small and Andrew Taylor, features interviews with a wide range of music industry superstars who reveal how they broke into the big time.

At least two sources for written job descriptions exist. One is the excellent publication from the Society of Professional Audio Recording Services (SPARS) entitled *SPARS Occupational Handbook*. The book includes detailed descriptions of each job required at a modern music recording or post production facility. The second is the book referenced earlier, *Career Opportunities in the Music Industry*.

Another way to find out the details of a particular career path is to network with professionals working in the business. *[We'll look more closely at networking in chapter 14.]* Depending on what jobs you are aspiring to, most likely there are working professionals in your area with whom you can make contact. Although this type of research requires more effort on your part, the quality and quantity of information, along with the ability to ask specific questions, makes this a far more valuable resource than simply reading.

Once again, if you are enrolled in a school program in the recording arts, ask your faculty and fellow students to keep you posted on professionals who may be coming to school to speak or give clinics. Also constantly seek out industry folk who have been helpful in the past in placing student as interns. ◉

WORKSHOP 2:
Your Dream Sheet

This workshop is a series of questions to help you do a basic self-assessment of where you hope to go and what you hope to accomplish in the music business. It should be considered a living document, much like your resume, kept on a computer disk and updated regularly.

Fill it out on a word processor or on a few sheets of lined paper now. When you complete the workshop, print it out and put it into the "My Journal" section of your career book. Mark your career book calendar six months ahead to read and update your dream sheet with the information you have learned in the interim.

Keep the earlier copies of your dream sheets so you can see how your perspectives evolve over time. A commentary is provided on the pages following the dream sheet, but don't look at it until you've completed all the questions in the workshop the first time.

1. What attracts you to a career in the music and recording industry?

2. List, in order of preference, the three jobs you would most like to be doing in the MRI?

   A.

   B.

   C.

3. Where do you want to be career-wise in five years? In ten years?

4. Where do you want to be personally and financially (salary range, own home, married/single/family, relocation) in five years? In ten years?

5. How much money do you think you could earn in the next one to two years if you landed any of the three jobs you listed above in question 2? Write down your best guess in the form of annual income.

   A.

   B.

   C.

6. Identify and list up to three jobs in which you have felt most fulfilled.

   A.

   B.

   C.

7. For each one, identify specifically what made you feel fulfilled.

   A.

   B.

   C.

8. Identify and list up to three jobs in which you have felt the least fulfilled.

   A.

   B.

   C.

9. For each one, identify specifically what made you feel unfulfilled.

   A.

   B.

   C.

10. Pick the number-one company for whom you would like to work today. Imagine you are being considered for a plum internship opportunity at that company. Write a paragraph explaining what attributes make you the best candidate for the internship.

11. State the single, most important thing you hope to gain from a career in the music industry.

Dream Sheet Commentary

Question 1: Knowing what attracts you to a career in the MRI is important to help you prioritize the various options and choices you will be faced with during your career evolution.

Question 2: These are jobs that you need to begin researching in order to determine the skills, job prospects, and earning potential for each.

Question 3: Time waits for no one. Setting goals that include a rough timeline is an important part of developing your career successfully. You must also confirm that your objectives and timeline are realistic as you meet working professionals. Revise your objectives as you uncover the story behind the jobs that interest you most.

Question 4: It's a fact that your career development will require a number of years of dues-paying: working long hours for low wages in often under-appreciated positions. Find out what people doing the jobs you aspire to do are earning as their career evolves.

Question 5: You may be surprised to learn that many low-level positions in the MRI pay about the same as working in a restaurant. Find out which career areas offer the best opportunities for advancement and salary growth. The best way to find out is to speak with working professionals. The polite way to ask is to inquire what the "salary range" is for a specific job.

Questions 6–9: Hopefully you have had a job that you excelled in, one that made you feel that your contributions were important to the success of the company. Likewise, you may have also suffered through "the job from hell." Reviewing the high and low points of jobs is another important step in assessing what kinds of tasks and duties you have been successful at. Finding the job you love and can excel in is often the most direct path to career and financial success. Going through this exercise will also help you discuss this area in a job interview.

Question 10: If you can't articulate your passion for a career in the music industry, you likely will fail to make a lasting impression on your future boss. Every performer, manager, or producer I know drives himself or herself relentlessly to be the absolute best.

Question 11: Is it money, power, fame, or artistic fulfillment? Knowing this will also help you reach decisions when your career comes to the inevitable forks in the road.

Analyzing Job Descriptions

There is no better way to gauge your readiness for a particular job than to look over a detailed job description or job profile. Let's look at one job profile for a record label intern, reprinted from *Career Opportunities in the Music Industry*.[1]

RECORD LABEL INTERN

Career Profile

Duties: Performing tasks in specific departments of a record company while learning the business under the direction of management.

Alternate Title: Trainee

Salary Range: \$0–\$15,000

Employment Prospects: Fair

Advancement Prospects: Good

Best Geographical Locations for Position: New York City, Los Angeles, and Nashville

Prerequisites:

Education or Training: High school diploma minimum; other requirements depend on position

Experience: No experience required

Special Skills and Personality Traits: Eagerness to learn, brightness, aggressiveness, knowledge of music and/or recording business, other skills, dependent on specific position

Career Ladder:

- Clerical position
- Student intern
- Staffer in department

Position Description

An intern working in a record company will perform many of the same duties as other people on staff. The intern works under the supervision of a department head, manager, or director. One of the advantages of obtaining an internship in a specific department is that the individual has the opportunity to learn the ropes from experienced people.

There are interns in almost every department of a record company. In certain companies, one becomes an intern in a single department. In others, the individual's internship involves working in various departments of the company. Duties will depend on the department to which one is assigned. For instance, an intern working in the publicity/press relations department may address invitations to press parties, make calls to check whether various people will be attending press parties, and help make arrangements for the press function. As he or she gains experience, the intern might begin writing press releases, attending meetings to work out publicity campaigns, or calling the media to discuss a good story.

[1] From *Career Opportunities in the Music Industry, Third Edition* by Shelly Field. Copyright ©1995 by Shelly Field. Reprinted by permission of Facts on File, Inc.

An intern working in the marketing department might work on consumer research surveys, tabulate data, and/or call radio stations and the trades with information about the number of records sold in a specific market. As time goes on, the intern may learn to develop marketing campaigns, go out with field reps, or help the director create a sales incentive program.

The intern usually begins by handling a lot of the tedious work that no one else wants to do. As he or she becomes more experienced, the intern learns how to perform more difficult tasks. Only the simplest of projects is performed without supervision.

Whether or not the intern is getting paid a salary, he or she is expected to function like a paid employee. This includes arriving to work on time and not taking time off unnecessarily. It is to the intern's advantage to learn as much as possible through instruction, asking questions and just working in a hands-on situation.

The individual is responsible to the supervisor or department head to which he or she is assigned. If the intern is using the internship as part of a college experience, a paper on the work experience may be expected.

A good intern has a fairly good chance of becoming a member of the company staff after the internship has concluded.

Salaries

Interns may work and not earn a penny. If they do earn a salary, it is usually quite small. An individual who has obtained an internship through a college might college credit for his or her work. If the person is working as an intern and is lucky enough to receive a salary, it probably would range from $5,000 to $15,000.

Employment Prospects

Despite the low pay or even lack of pay, many people want to work as interns. Internships can be found in almost any department of every major record company. Smaller labels tend to offer fewer alternatives.

Although many of these internship programs may be located directly through the record company, there are a number that can be obtained through schools and colleges in return for credit and hands-on experience.

Advancement Prospects

One of the major reasons so many people become interns in this industry is that it almost guarantees a job in the record company. After all the training and instruction, the company most likely will want to keep the intern in its employ. The person must, of course, be a good employee and learn the trade. Interns can advance their careers very quickly in most departments. They may first be promoted to staffers, and then become coordinators, supervisors, or directors in various departments.

Education and Training

To become an intern in a record company the only education required may be a high school diploma. If an individual is currently in college, he or she may be able to have the school set up an internship program with a company for college credit. The person may be working toward a degree in any subject that can be made relevant to a semester or summer in a record company. Majors might include business, advertising, music, communications, journalism, the social sciences, pre-law, etc.

Experience/Skills/Personality

Interns do not really need any experience. What is required is the desire to enter the record industry and an eagerness to learn all about it.

Individuals who are chosen to be interns are generally bright and aggressive and have pleasant personalities. A knowledge of music and/or the recording business is a plus.

A student or recent graduate is likely to start their career path working in a clerical position before moving to an internship. If you work hard, an opportunity may open up to become a staffer in one of the various departments in the label. Locate a copy of *Career Opportunities in the Music Industry* and review other listings for record label positions such as **Staff Publicist** or **Promotions Staffer**. Each will reference its own career ladder.

If you're serious about a career in the music and recording industry you must unearth this type of detailed job and earnings information. If you haven't done the research and you just blunder along, how do you know you're going to get where you want? How will you know a job has the potential to earn what you want to earn?

TIPS FOR ENTRY:

- If you are in college, the school may know of some intern positions in record companies. If the school has a music business program, merchandising degree, or offers courses, it might have an internship program already established with a record company.
- Contact record labels to see if they offer intern programs or if you can develop an internship.
- If you live in one of the music capitals, you might want to visit the record companies personally to see if you can get an internship in one of the departments.
- Interns are often chosen from the ranks of clerical workers in the office. Talk to the head of the department with which you want to work.

Now let's look at an actual job description for a position creating music and sound effects for a computer game developer.

A job description such as this one lays out a road map. With a job description in hand, take an inventory of the skills and knowledge required to successfully fill the position, and determine the areas in which you may be lacking knowledge. ⊙

Job Title: Game sound designer, full-time, salaried position

Position Summary: This person will work with software designers and senior sound staff to create music and sounds for the company's latest products. In addition to maintaining the highest possible audio production values, the sound designer will be responsible for adhering to the stylistic approach determined for the specific product. Ability to complete work within established timeline is required.

Job Responsibilities:

- Edit sound effects and synchronize with animation and other interactive elements of the product
- Edit dialog
- Compose music segments, songs, and cues to enhance the product
- Arrange music for the types of synthesizers utilized in PC and Mac CPUs as well as general MIDI synthesizers
- Review sounds and music to be developed with product development team and software engineers to ensure playability
- Stay current on various developments in MIDI playback systems for computer applications

Qualifications:

- Ability to compose music in a wide range of musical styles.
- Four-year degree in music or equivalent practical musical knowledge that can be demonstrated through composition and arranging examples.
- Extensive experience arranging music for various types of synthesizers including those commonly used in the general MIDI specification. Thorough knowledge of synthesis techniques, patch editing, and sequencing software.
- Familiarity with digital sound editing tools such as Sound Designer and Sound Forge. Strong understanding of the principles of digital audio and the physical properties of sound. Must know the basic sound properties of the various families of musical instruments (strings, brass, woodwinds, percussion, etc.).
- Experience with Macintosh, Windows, and MS-DOS computers required. Basic knowledge of computer language such as C++ helpful but not mandatory. Practical experience in a recording studio environment is a plus.

The successful candidate for this position will already be well along on their career path. They will have a strong music and composition background and be well-versed in MIDI. Note that although composing is generally a solitary pursuit, this position requires frequent interaction with other members of the software development team.

Your Marketable Skill Set

I'm going to introduce you now to "skill set assessment"—a technique I've developed to help you work toward your career goals. It will help you identify your marketable skills. For instance, if you are fluent in a second language, that linguistic proficiency is a component of your unique marketable skill set. Some of you may already be well along the road to developing a strong set of these skills. Others may be at the very beginning of the process.

Your marketable skill set will be composed of two groups: first, your **foundation skills**, the ones you'll need for any job in today's world; and second, **job-specific skills** that will be required for you to excel in a specific position in the MRI.

For those who have already developed a number of these skills, jump in and learn how to assess your marketable skill set against the ones required for the positions you are seeking. However, if you are a rookie at the beginning of your skill set development, don't tackle building your marketable skill set just yet. Instead, read over this section and remember to come back to it *after* you have spent some time in school or in an on-the-job-training situation such as an industry internship. Then see how your evolving skills stack up against what you have discovered is needed for a particular MRI job. Otherwise the exercise may prove frustrating to you.

To increase your "hire-ability," your marketable skill set should be made up of the skills that a prospective employer will look at and say, "We can use their particular set of skills around here." That's because when an employer considers whether or not to hire you, they're basically trying to answer one question, "What is this person going to do to make my life easier?"

That's the question you must clearly answer when you set out to create a strong resume or go for a job interview. What are you going to be able to do to make your next boss's life better and easier, and make the company more efficient and profitable? Your marketable skill set lays out what you're able to do to help your prospective employer.

WORKSHOP 3:
Foundation Skills Assessment

Taking an inventory of your own marketable skills is a key step in your career development. In today's fast-paced entertainment world, foundation skills are a prerequisite to being considered for most jobs.

Rate your foundation skills below.

	STRONG	MODERATE	NEEDS WORK
Reading and writing	☐	☐	☐
Verbal communication	☐	☐	☐
Listening	☐	☐	☐
Understanding and following instructions	☐	☐	☐
Observing and assessing situations and problems	☐	☐	☐
Decision-making	☐	☐	☐
Computer word processing	☐	☐	☐
Computer database ability	☐	☐	☐
Computer spreadsheet ability	☐	☐	☐
Internet navigation and research	☐	☐	☐

The first six skills are interpersonal skills that most people will have developed some proficiency at through school, social, and business situations. The last four relate specifically to computers and the Internet. Today's job seeker must have a basic knowledge of those functions in order to be a productive member of any music or recording industry company.

If you believe you could benefit from strengthening your interpersonal skills, you should see a counselor at your school or local community college and investigate what type of class will help you develop your skills in this area. Speech, language, and writing classes are a few that can help. For computer skills and applications, community colleges offer a low-cost means to develop satisfactory basic skills in each of the four crucial computing areas mentioned in the list above.

Analyzing a Sample Marketable Skill Set

As an example, let's look at a marketable skill set for an aspiring recording engineer. (Again, remember to look before you jump. Even if your chosen career path is not in the studio as a recording engineer, it is valuable for you to review this marketable skill set carefully. It will cue you as to the level of job detail and responsibility to research and review for each specific MRI career you are interested in pursuing.)

MARKETABLE SKILL SET FOR AUDIO ENGINEER

Foundation Skills

- Reading/writing/following instructions
- Having the ability to communicate clearly
- Being able to stay calm and cool
- Having basic computer skills

Job-Specific Skills

- Critical listening skills
- Audio expertise
- A good "bedside manner"

Here's a breakdown of the critical skills that today's recording engineer must possess or develop.

Foundation Skills

1. **You have to be able to read, write, and (yes,) follow instructions.** Why is it critical in a recording studio to follow instructions?

   Well, you could damage the equipment. You're working with people's master recordings that are the result of thousands of hours and perhaps hundreds of thousands of dollars' investment. More importantly, following instructions means that the studio, the first engineer, or the head tech can say, "Tim, go take care of this for me." That person is not always going to have the time to sit and coach Tim through that activity. So they must be confident that Tim is going to be able to listen, integrate what the request is, and get it properly accomplished. If that's the case, then Tim is a person a studio will want to employ. Because they can teach, mentor, and coach him, they can move him ahead on the career track. They can develop a valuable employee for the firm. Following instructions is critical to learning how to work successfully in any type of a studio or production environment.

2. **The ability to communicate clearly.** Many times when I was engineering a recording session, the producer or an artist said, "It just isn't right. I don't know what it is. It isn't getting me." We often spent hours trying to find out what it would take to "get them." Or you may find yourself working with musicians from another culture or a new genre of music. You have to be able to communicate clearly in order to be as efficient as possible in the recording studio. Many of the delays and problems encountered in the studio are the result of poor or complete lack of communication skills.

   Knowing when to communicate is also crucial. I mentioned earlier the psychology skills an engineer must develop. Well, you've got to learn when to tell somebody, "This isn't working, what if we tried something like…" You also must know when to keep quiet and let the recording artist figure it out for themselves.

3. **The ability to stay calm and cool.** Do you think that artists get emotional in the studio? They're pouring out their whole persona into their performance for everyone to hear. So they do get emotional. A capable engineer must know how to stay cool when an artist vents their frustration. I've been in sessions where fights have broken out in the mix room between management and the band. People have actually taken a poke at each other. Generally, that's not conducive to the creative process. You have to stay cool, and you have to remember your job is to keep the project on track.

4. **Having basic computer skills.** How much computer knowledge do you need to make it as a recording engineer? The more you know, the more valuable you'll be. You absolutely have to know basics like how to type a letter with word processing software. You must know what a database is, and how it works. You must know spreadsheet functions so you can use the computer to add, subtract, multiply, and divide. You must be comfortable with those three basic applications.

   As mentioned earlier, you can get adequate computer "basic training" at your local community college. A basic computer class covering these applications will teach the fundamentals.

If you walk into your first day as an intern or a gofer and your boss tells you, "Go log these fifty tapes into the tape library," and he points you to the computer and you can't figure it out—you're out.

Should you be proficient on the Macintosh or the PC platform? Good question. Those using the computer for composing, sequencing, and making music tend to use the Mac. The folks who are counting the beans, checking whether the gear has been fixed or not, and managing the business are running PCs.

It's helpful to know both. All of the computer editing software for sound and music initially was Mac-based. However, during the last few years, the PC is coming on strong with respect to music software.

Job-Specific Skills

5. **Having critical listening skills.** When I was working as a producer, a computer company came to me and said, "We made this sample floppy disk that has some musical instrument sounds on it that people play when they buy their computer and plug it in. It shows musical instrument graphics on the screen and then plays that instrument's sounds. We're getting quite a few back with complaints about the sound."

So they sent me one of the disks and we loaded it up and played the sound file. It was a little tiny sound file, at a very low sampling rate. (Remember what the video game "Pong" sounded like?) And it sounded like a chain saw. I told them, "Well, we don't have the original sound source to do a comparison, but it kind of sounds like a chain saw."

And they said, "Oh no, no, that's a clarinet!" So the people who had purchased the computers were seeing a picture of a kid playing a clarinet on their computer screen, but they were hearing this chain saw sound. It had been sampled with so much distortion that it didn't even sound like a musical instrument anymore. So in the studio, no one was listening to see if the musical instrument samples really sounded like instruments! That's an extreme—but real—example of how critical listening skills could have saved a lot of time, money, and headaches.

If you have not listened to or experienced music in an acoustic environment, you may not know what you're listening for, and you're going to have problems as an engineer. So, you've got to listen to music. And not just recorded music, because recorded music is an illusion of a performance, even if it is a live performance. The well-respected engineer and producer Bruce Swedien encourages up-and-coming engineers to get out and experience every type of music there is in a concert setting, from rock to opera to string quartets to jazz, folk, big band, and blues. Bruce reminds young engineers that records are sonic illusions or sound paintings. In order to become a competent engineer you have to build up a library in your mind of what instruments sound like naturally—one at a time and in ensembles. Truer words were never spoken.

View your time spent developing listening skills just as you would doing homework. Go out once a week or once a month. Listen to classical, listen to jazz. If you want to be a recording engineer you've got to have heard it all. Because one day you're going to be in a session and somebody is going to come in with an accordion, a didgeridoo, a harp, or a banjo. You should know how each instrument should sound.

One day I was engineering a jingle session and the producer brought in a gentleman who said, "I'm a whistler." That was one of the hardest things I ever had to record in my engineering career. I had to experiment with a number of different setups to get it right. But I started by just standing in the room with him and moving around to assess how he sounded in different spots in the room as he whistled, before I even plugged in a mic.

6. **Having audio expertise.** You have to develop a thorough knowledge of audio, such as signal flow, phase, and microphone selection and placement. Whether you are self-taught or go to a recording school, you have to acquire the basic knowledge of how to make a recording, do overdubs, and handle a mixdown.

7. **Having a good "bedside manner."** That's the mood or tone that an engineer sets as they work with a client or artist on a session. Why is that important? The most successful studio engineers I know are the ones that create an environment that is conducive to getting creative work done. The finest equipment doesn't mean a thing if the vibe is not good in the studio. Even if you have a $750,000 recording console, what good is it if when the artist walks in, he or she doesn't feel comfortable? If artists are cared for, even pampered, a good engineer will capture that artist's best performance.

So now you know the basic marketable skill set required to have a solid career in engineering. When a student asks me, "*Keith, what do I have to do to get a job as an engineer?*" Well, get those seven things together. The first six you can learn in school. The seventh, there's only one way to learn it: experience. You've got to sit down in a session—watch other experienced engineers work—in order to observe and learn what's good about their bedside manners. That's why it's a good idea to start out at an established studio that provides some training or internships. That way, you can learn from pros.

It's also very helpful if you've played music, can read music, or are conversant with the musical language. Know enough about musical structure to understand what forte, ritardando, and the "B" section of a musical chart represent. If you are booked to record a Dixieland band next week, go to a record store or online and buy a couple of well-regarded Dixieland records. It won't break your bank account to spend a few bucks and a couple of hours listening to them to understand how the instruments blend and how the solos sit in the mix.

Then when that Dixieland band walks in and you meet the musicians, you've already got a point of departure to build a rapport. You can say, "Yeah, I bought a Turk Murphy recording, and I was checking out how these guys sounded together." The band will think, "My engineer took the time to learn something about what we do. All right! Let's make a good recording." ⊙

WORKSHOP 4:
Job-Specific Skills Assessment

Look back at your dream sheet from Workshop 2, which should be copied and resident in the "My Journal" section of your career book.

Question 2 asked you to identify three specific MRI jobs that interested you. For each job, it will be up to you to uncover what specific key skills are necessary to enter that career path. Use this workshop exercise to log the skills that you uncover and to determine which ones you need to develop. Photocopy this page for each job so you can start to assess what job-specific skills you'll need to build on top of your foundation skills.

Marketable Skill Set: Job-Specific Skills Assessment

Job Title: ______________________________

Skill List	HAVE	NEED
____________________	☐	☐
____________________	☐	☐
____________________	☐	☐
____________________	☐	☐
____________________	☐	☐
____________________	☐	☐
____________________	☐	☐
____________________	☐	☐

You may not be able to identify all the skills required for a specific job all at once. Keep each sheet updated as you speak with working professionals, review job skills, and read interviews with persons doing the job you are researching. In a very short time, you'll have most of the key skills identified.

Next, identify the career progression in the chosen field you are researching.

Entry-level position: ______________________________

Advances to: ______________________________

Advances to: ______________________________

Advances to: ______________________________

Advances to: ______________________________

Here is a sample completed job-specific skill assessment sheet for a recording engineer job seeker named Jan Carlson.

MARKETABLE SKILL SET:
JOB-SPECIFIC SKILLS ASSESSMENT FOR JAN CARLSON

Job Title: Music Recording Engineer

Skill List	HAVE	NEED
Critical listening skills	☒	☐
Practical audio knowledge, signal flow	☒	☐
Recording session experience	☐	☒
Knowledge of music and instruments	☒	☐
Microphone and mic placement knowledge	☐	☒
Analog record/edit skills	☐	☒
Digital record/edit skills	☒	☐
Computer, MIDI, and music software skills	☒	☐
Good bedside manner with clients	☐	☒

Next, identify the career progression in the chosen field you are researching.

Entry-level position: Gofer, Studio Runner or Assistant
Advances to: Tape Copy or Dubbing
Advances to: Assistant or Second Engineer
Advances to: First Engineer
Advances to: Elite Engineer or Engineer/Producer

Researching Various Job Skill Sets

At a record label, if you start as an administrative assistant, you may next move up to A&R assistant. Then you move ahead to an A&R coordinator. Next, perhaps you do some fieldwork or advance work with the promotion team for one of your artists. The book referenced earlier, *Career Opportunities in the Music Industry* by Shelly Field, provides an invaluable resource for learning the various rungs on many job paths. This volume describes jobs in various fields, job prospects, and paths of advancement and salary ranges. It also outlines what skills you will need in a particular job. It is a great way to research a job, especially if you are unable to locate a practicing professional in each area of interest.

Using the marketable skill set workshops (Foundation Skills and Job-Specific Skills) in combination with suggestions from Field's book will allow you to assess quickly and realistically how far along towards a particular job you may be. Don't worry if at first you don't appear to have some of the skills required. Few of us did when we started out, and just identifying the marketable skills you will need to develop puts you a step ahead of the wannabes who spend their time dreaming about the industry job they "wish" they could obtain. You'll already have identified the skills that will make your own particular MRI career dream a reality.

Use these workshops over and over. When something new occurs to you, you think, "What about Internet radio? What about publishing rights—perhaps I can go into that?" Never throw out your completed sheets. Put them in your career binder for future reference.

At the bottom of the job-specific workshop page is the particular career path. While you're completing this part of the workshop, it's also time to do some basic salary research.

When it comes to your earning potential in various jobs, don't be ignorant. Talk to people in the field, and look at what is available in print. You have to be able to survive while you build your career. If you haven't done your earning homework and then find out firsthand that you can't get by on what the lower rungs of your career ladder pay, you may be setting yourself up for early failure. Your completed marketable skill set workshops will come in handy when it comes time to build your resume. Knowing what skills are required to be an A&R assistant will help you craft a resume and cover letter that demonstrate that you have invested in building the necessary skills to tackle the job duties required for that position.

A final point about your research and completion of the marketable skill set workshops. Although you can find a lot of valuable information from books, I strongly encourage you to then review the workshop data with a working professional in that field. It's important to validate your findings not only on salary ranges, but also on key skills and the career path as you have researched it. Checking and verifying these facts will help you to attain some peace of mind as you begin the career journey ahead. ⊙

Building a Winning Resume

The most important document you will develop over the course of your career is your resume. Whether it's a one-pager when you're getting your career started or a two-pager for a grizzled veteran, your written resume has to effectively communicate everything you can bring to the workplace. It must stand out from a pile of resumes on the desk of a potential employer.

Resume Example: Take a look at the sample resume below, modeled closely on that of one of my former students who is now working in the audio post production industry.

This is a *chronological resume*. What does that mean? It's laid out in the order of time, from the most recent accomplishments to the older ones.

The "Other" Resume—A Functional Resume

Another way to present yourself is via a *functional resume*. It lists accomplishments in the order you feel best represents your qualifications for a particular career path. In which instance would you consider developing a functional rather than a chronological resume? Usually, it's most appropriate if you either have gaps in your timeline or you're changing careers.

Maybe you've worked as a legal clerk for the last five years. Prior to that, you worked in radio, and you're ready to get back to broadcasting. You don't want the very first thing a screener reads under experience to be your clerking for a large law firm. Because when they get that over at K-101, they're going to think, "H-m-m-m, she's a law clerk wanting to get back into the business." Probable destination for that resume: shredder pile!

In this scenario, use a functional resume to highlight your skills. In the radio/law example above, you lead with your radio experience and accomplishments and list your legal work later in the resume. That's the difference between chronological and functional. But I would estimate that more than 90 percent of the time, a chronological resume is the best approach in the early stages of your MRI career. Examples of a functional resume can be found in the Payne book mentioned in the Resource section.

In the sample resume, **job objective** is narrowed down to one line. Candidates at the entry level should be saying, "I'm here to learn, please teach me." The position sought in our sample

JAN N. CARLSON

36362 Shining Star Court, Fremont, CA 94538 • (H) 510 767-1111 • jncarlson@yahoo.com

Objective

To obtain an entry-level position as an assistant sound engineer in the film/music industry

Work experience

Staff Engineer, Bill Smythe Creative Services

1995–1998

Oakland, CA

Assisted leading composer of film scores with engineering, session set-up and all aspects of studio productions. Engineered over 12 film and video sound tracks. Planned and executed upgrade of new MIDI studio including drawings, wiring and installation, saving the cost of hiring an outside installation firm.

Technical Manager, Audio, San Francisco State University Technical Services

1997–1998

San Francisco, CA

Coordinated all sound reinforcement work done on campus. Worked with artists and management to determine sound reinforcement needs for each show and supervised set up, operation and tear down for 52 shows. Set up maintenance tracking system and student repair teams to lower amount of equipment out of service and speed up repairs, resulting in increased productivity of department and letter of commendation.

Education

San Francisco State University

1994–1999

San Francisco, CA

BA, Broadcast and Electronic Communication Arts

Other Skills

- Own and operate 8-track ADAT–MIDI home studio for personal projects
- Ten years experience playing the guitar
- Ability to read, write and understand music
- Working knowledge of MIDI and Macintosh sequencing software, knowledge of Macintosh, Windows and MS-DOS

Professional memberships

- Associate member of NARAS
- Student member of AES, Treasurer of SFSU Chapter

Hobbies & Interests

- Backpacking, camping, fishing, and collecting blues recordings

References available upon request.

resume, assistant sound engineer, means they are looking for a specific job in the film/music industry. It's broad but not *too* broad. They didn't say "the record business, recording." As you read further down this resume, you can see whether or not this person's **work experience** supports the career path listed in their job objective. In this case, it does. They've already taken some important career development steps. They've assisted in composing film scores and have done engineering and rudimentary sound design. Their resume points to a likely career path in audio production for film and video sound tracks.

This person's **education** is listed as well as some interests and activities. They stated their degree as briefly as possible, listing the school, the course of study, degree conferred, and when they were enrolled. You need not list anything else. Specifics about course work completed can be shared during an interview, if necessary.

Other skills are an important category on this resume. For this person, it's a clear-cut way to list some of their other marketable skills, demonstrating experience with technology and music.

Two affiliations are noted under **professional memberships**. A few **hobbies and interests** are listed on the sample resume to help the candidate stand out from the competition.

The sample resume's overall presentation is very solid, tight, and has an extremely clean look. It uses white space effectively, thereby avoiding the overly crowded, difficult-to-read document many students develop. Toss it in a pile of resumes and it's got name recognition as well as simplicity to help it stand out.

Don't copy this resume directly. Rather, look at what is in it, the phrases used, and how it clearly states a case that this person would be a valuable asset to a company in the music, film sound, or recording industry. References to this sample resume will be included over the following chapters, so leave a bookmark near it so you can quickly flip back to it.

Making Your Resume a "Hit"

There are two sayings about songwriting that apply equally to your resume development. One, that "a song hasn't been written until it's been rewritten." And another, that songwriting is "10 percent inspiration and 90 percent perspiration." Just like a hit song, the best resumes have appeal, hooks, and are very easy to digest. They leave the reader with a memorable impression. They are compact and use the minimum number of words to make the maximum impression. Accomplishing these goals requires a serious investment of time and commitment. As your resume evolves, you will continually massage it, trying to figure out a way to boil a paragraph down to ten words. Tighten your career objective, if you're going to use one, from thirty words to twelve words. That's the nature of the task.

A colleague of mine who is a senior human resources executive once shared an interesting fact with me. I had always been under the impression that the people who screen resumes, especially at larger firms, looked for the strongest resumes of those submitted. I was surprised to learn that it's often actually the opposite case.

In many larger companies, a resume screener's job is to look for mistakes: to take as many resumes as they can and justifiably put them in the shredder. Why? "This one is full of misspellings." (Buzzzzzz… goes the shredder.) "This one says she only will work in A&R." (Buzzzzzzzz.) "This one says he wants to be the president of the label." (Buzzzzzzz.)

In a large organization, the resume screener's job is not to pick the strongest resume; it's to leave a pile of nonoffensive resumes for their supervisor's review. That's why you cannot afford the slightest error or mistake on your resume. It can quickly eliminate you from consideration.

So your first task in the resume quest is to commit yourself to developing a resume without negatives and errors. You'd be surprised at how many resumes I have seen over the years in which people stated, "I really hated this job, so I quit," or something to that effect, right on their resume! We've all had a job we didn't like, but please, don't put that on your resume.

It's critically important to make sure that your resume is read and proofread by you and others. What does it say about you and your attention to the details of life and work if your resume includes typos, spelling, or grammar mistakes?

Your resume must be compact, concise, typed or word-processed, well laid-out, and clean looking. If you have access to a computer you can generally lay it out on your own. If you don't, go to a shop such as Kinko's and rent computer time. Type up your resume *after* you have developed a hand-written draft and proofed it (with the help of some extra eyes) a few times. For a small fee, many copy shops will sell you a floppy disk, so you can save it on that disk, keep it with you, and update it regularly. Your resume should be a tool you update and improve as your MRI career develops.

Never Underestimate the Power of a Strong Resume

A well-crafted resume is a strong statement of why you are a leading candidate for a prospective opening. In many cases, it will be the *only* chance you have to sell yourself to your future boss.

Let's say there's a job opportunity in New York (and you live elsewhere), and you hear about it through your network. What's the first step you take? You should call up and confirm that the company is looking for someone with some of the same qualifications you possess. They'll say, "Send us your resume." Well, are you going to fly there to give it to them? Probably not, unless you're heading for a senior level position.

You're going to mail, fax, or e-mail them your resume. This piece of paper represents you: your life, your skills, your value, your net worth, your marketable skills. Will it be the best, strongest, tightest document you can create or a quickie that you copied out of a resume book you picked up the night before?

In this same scenario, another candidate simply mails in a naked resume. You sent in a resume *and* a well-written cover letter. Your cover letter is another opportunity for you to highlight the key points on your resume, point out things that you have done that have created value in the past, and to show that you have some knowledge of the company and the position they're looking to fill. All these things will separate you from the pack, and help you avoid the hungry resume shredder. So always make the time to write a solid cover letter. (You'll learn how to craft a knockout cover letter in a few chapters.)

Your Recipe for a Top-Notch Resume

It's time to roll up your sleeves and develop a resume that will set you apart from the competition. As you read the following pages, refer back to our sample resume frequently to see how it stacks up to these criteria. After reading the building blocks of your successful resume, you'll do a workshop to get you started crafting the first draft of your own hit resume.

Elements of Your Resume

Identity: The first thing your resume must denote is who you are—literally. You have to clearly and boldly state your identity. Your name must be at the top. How big should you make it? I recommend 14- to 18-point type if you're using 10- to 12-point in the body of your resume. Visualize twenty resumes on a table. If your identity is bigger than the rest, but not too big, you've got a little bit of an edge.

Should you use distinctive fonts? No. Often, when it comes to resumes, especially at larger companies like major record labels, your resume will be scanned. And if you used a bizarre font called "Antediluvian," your name may appear as a black splotch when scanned. So it's good to rely on standard fonts like Times, Helvetica, or Courier.

The only exception might be if you are applying for a position as a graphic designer, in which case it may be appropriate to show a tad more design sense in your resume. But even then, don't go overboard. Let your portfolio show your creative flair, and let your resume explain verbally why you are the best candidate for that graphic artist position.

Job objective: The job objective answers the question, what do you aspire to do? For an individual who aspires to become an established songwriter a job objective might be:

Sample Job Objective
To obtain an entry-level position at a music publishing company to learn more about the publishing industry.

That's a good job objective statement. And you can adapt your objective from opportunity to opportunity. That's the beauty of word processors. That's why you've got your floppy disk with your resume on it.

What if you don't have a specific job objective yet? Then identify a segment of the industry that you have an interest in, such as A&R, sound reinforcement, or artist management, and start with that.

Sample Job Objective
To secure an entry-level position at an artist management company.

I think it's important to list an objective. If you know you want to be in the studio business but you're not sure where, you should say so.

Sample Job Objective
To land an entry-level position in an established recording studio to expand my recording knowledge and skills.

Although it's generic, it gives the reader a sense that the candidate has a goal in mind.

Experience: This part of your resume gives you the opportunity to detail some of your accomplishments. Many people get intimidated when it comes to listing experience on their resume. The simple rule of thumb on listing experience on your resume is to emphasize your strongest accomplishments, no matter where you were employed. As your career evolves on the MRI path of your choice, then your experience should reflect your career development in your chosen area.

THE SAGA OF THE PIZZA MAN

One of my former students started working in the eleventh grade for a pizza parlor in San Francisco. He was just finishing up his four-year degree in broadcasting and had been working at the pizza shop for six or seven years. At that time he was assistant manager with fiscal responsibilities, hiring, and training people, etc. He came to me and said, "My goal is to work in a recording studio, so I'm not going to mention this stuff," i.e., his pizza business experience.

I replied, "You're shortchanging yourself if you omit this valuable experience. Look at all the skills you've developed. You're fiscally responsible, and you hired and managed a staff of ten people. You've developed menus. Those are all important business skills. Put them down on your resume. You don't have to write volumes, but include what you've accomplished that's noteworthy and that contributed to the success of your employer. Every business owner wants to hire someone who has proven to be a responsible employee."

Never forget to tell your prospective employer what problems you solved or profits you helped create in a previous job. The majority of your competitors will only list the dates and title of the jobs they held. Too bad for them! They miss a tremendous opportunity that you ***must*** take advantage of to explain the ***value*** you created in your previous and current job.

Education: How important is it in our industry? Increasingly so. Programs such as Music Production and Engineering at Berklee College of Music in Boston, and the Certificate Program in the Music and Recording Industry offered by San Francisco State University are outstanding. Studios, labels, management companies, and other firms that recruit entry-level employees rely on programs such as these, as well as two- and four-year programs granting degrees and specialized trade schools.

When it comes time to start your job search, your educational background will definitely help you. What if you don't have an education in the MRI field? It's still important to list your educational qualifications. If you have a high school diploma, list it. If you took college courses but didn't graduate, specify the general area of study and number of years or credits completed successfully.

Prospective employers want to know that you are literate. Remember that being able to read, write, and follow directions are important components of your marketable skill set. Documenting your education and background is important. Unfortunately, I've received far too many resumes that listed no educational accomplishments. That's a mistake. Today one must list educational background to be considered seriously for almost any position.

Background and interests: Why would you want to put these down on your resume? Because more often than not, landing your dream job in the music biz means building a rapport with the person who will hire or work with you. And if you have some common interests, be they antique cars, home-brewed beer, or cycling, it's liable to not only go a long way by breaking the ice, but more importantly, separating you from your competition.

Background and interests provide an excellent means to differentiate you from the pack. Let's say you have a huge album collection of a specific genre of music, and the label at which you're applying is developing artists in that genre. You learned of the label through a few articles you discovered in *Billboard* or *Spin* magazine, so there appears to be a nice fit. Your interest in this genre of music may become a plus if you are applying for a position at that label.

Background and interests provide you with a chance to strike a chord with someone. Let's say you're into backpacking and the person who is interviewing you is also a backpacker. Backgrounds and interests allow you to differentiate yourself.

Personal interviews are often a bit like the start of a recording session with a new artist. You and your interviewer may be a bit nervous. Your interests may prove to be a good icebreaker. And the fact that you have some interests beyond your career goals is a healthy sign that you value a well-rounded life.

Avoid mentioning any interests that are highly charged or political in nature. Stick with pursuits and interests that do not offer any chance to upset a prospective employer. Be careful to never lie or invent any information on your resume. Chances are it will come back to haunt you and in some cases may prove to be grounds for dismissal.

References: Should you list character references on your resume? The answer is no. You may, however, choose to add a line at the bottom, *references available upon request*. You must then remember to actually secure reliable references that will vouch for you, because they are likely to be called upon to do so.

Who makes a good reference? Anyone with whom you have worked in a professional capacity. If your experience so far has been only as a student, use your instructors. If you're really in a pinch, use anyone who knows you well, except for family. That's the only taboo on references. Attorney, minister, former boss at the pizza parlor: those are acceptable, too. At some point, you're going to need references, so start planning who will provide this important service for you and ask their permission to use them as a reference in your job search. Some interviewers don't ask for references. Companies are starting to do so more often, especially for positions of responsibility.

Progressive Career Growth

As your career and resume evolve, take the time to clearly delineate the various examples that show your progressive career growth. This is a prime indicator used by prospective employers to measure the development of a job applicant. Simply put, progressive career growth shows how you have advanced in job responsibility and value to your current and previous employers. It's also wise to point out your progressive growth career in cover letters that accompany any resume submissions.

Presentation: What about your resume's presentation? You should make it easy to read, and carefully check and re-check for spelling or grammar errors. As noted earlier, with respect to the sample resume, leave some white space. By that I mean do not cram the page so full of information that the reader's eye is overwhelmed; leave it a bit airy. You should also avoid colored paper and nonstandard fonts. If a resume comes in and it is so packed with words that the reader doesn't know where to start, you've got a major problem. If your resume is running long or looking crammed on a single page, go to another page. Better yet, get a friend, teacher, or mentor to help you edit it down. Leave somewhite space. I repeat that point, because it is so often ignored, but critically important in aiding your resume's view-ability.

If you are ready to vie for an entry-level position in the MRI, there is rarely a need for your resume to run any more than a single, well-organized page.

A Final Thought on Resume Editing

Students often inquire, "Should they revise or edit their resume for *each* job opportunity that they uncover as their job search gets into high gear?" The answer is, "No!"

I don't advise overhauling your resume for every single job opportunity because you're liable to stray from the carefully crafted document that you spent so much time developing. The basics of your education, your experience, and your talents will not change from opportunity to opportunity. And your basic qualifications and worth points (we'll get to those shortly) shouldn't change either. Over the arc of your career, measured in years, it will change—but not every month.

You might add a sentence here or there, and your job objective may certainly be edited to suit a specific opportunity, but the core of a well-crafted resume should rarely change. A well-crafted resume is a solid document that clearly states who you are. It unequivocally states what you've done—the scope of your accomplishments and the results to your previous and current employers. In your interview and cover letter, you can and should amplify specific skills and key accomplishments that are likely to excite your future boss.

If you're constantly doctoring up the basics of your resume, you're likely to introduce errors and more formatting problems. Once you have a strong resume that you are justifiably proud of, think twice before tampering with its basic elements. ⊙

WORKSHOP 5:
Beginning Your Resume

Take the following list and set it up in a word processor or on a blank sheet of lined paper.

Review this chapter's discussion and make the initial draft of the ideas and words that will grow into your own "hit" resume. Once you have some ideas and notes, then you'll be ready to start a first draft of your resume. This will help you avoid that sinking feeling many encounter when tackling your resume.

Identity: List your name, address, phone, and other contact information including fax and e-mail if applicable. Some students list school and home contact information.

Job Objective: Don't try to write the perfect job objective; instead, simply note a few of the job objectives you aspire to at this time. Most entry-level candidates have a number of dream careers they are interested in investigating. List as many as come to mind. Don't agonize over the wordsmithing now, as you will have time to perfect and fine-tune that later.

Work Experience: For now, list it all in chronological order. Include part-time and volunteer positions. Pay special attention to any jobs for which you received commendations, raises, promotions, or other identifiable accolades.

Education: Keep it short, but don't omit any training or internship that strengthens your resume.

Other Skills: Start a list of all the skills you can think of that may be valuable, especially skills such as foreign language proficiency, negotiating skills, and telephone and computer skills. Even the ability to drive a truck may prove handy. Once you have your list going, poll your close friends and family members to expand your list. Again, in this early phase of resume development, it's far better to have a wider range of choices and to narrow it down later.

Professional Memberships: If you don't have any professional affiliations yet, perhaps now is the time to do some homework and identify one or two organizations that may interest you. Even if you can't afford the dues, you could become involved as a volunteer.

Hobbies and Interests: Start with every one you have and pare down later.

References: Although you don't need your final list of three nonfamily character references yet, it's not too soon to identify who your top candidates will be.

Make Your Resume Sparkle with Worth Points

A "worth point" is a well-written, concise statement that will differentiate you from your competition. Worth points are worth their weight in gold, so take the time to learn how to incorporate them into your resume. Worth points demonstrate *why* you will be valuable to an employer. They make your resume shine and glisten.

Worth points clearly state *what* you accomplished and the *results* your actions created for your previous employer.

> ***Worth Point Example:***
> *Organized and managed volunteer student committee to raise funds for repair of homeless shelter, resulting in achieving 200 percent of financial goal.*

Notice that the example incorporates two action verbs in it, *organized* and *managed*. It also clearly states that your efforts exceeded the goal or expectation that was established before you tackled the job.

Notice the worth point statements in the model resume in the previous chapter.

> ***Worth Point Example:***
> *Planned and executed upgrade of new MIDI studio, including drawings, wiring, and installation, saving the cost of hiring an outside installation firm.*

That's a strong worth point that uses two powerful verbs, *planned* and *executed*. The resume could have simply stated, "installed a new MIDI studio," and missed a valuable opportunity to make a much stronger, active statement as to the value created for the previous employer.

A worth point is also included under the school job listed on the sample resume in the previous chapter.

> ***Worth Point Example:***
> *Set up maintenance tracking system and student repair teams to lower amount of equipment out of service and speed up repairs, resulting in increased productivity of department and letter of commendation.*

The studio manager who is looking at this resume carefully is likely to observe, "This person is technical enough so that I wouldn't have to contract out as much freelance technical help. I'd have more tech power in-house. And he has organized repair teams and kept equipment running."

That well-stated worth point is very likely to move the sample resume up near the top of the select pile of "must contact" resumes.

Use the workshop on the next page to develop a few of your own worth points.

WORKSHOP 6:
Worth Point Development

A "worth point" is a well-written, concise way to give yourself an edge when someone is reviewing your resume. Worth points demonstrate **why** *you will be valuable to a prospective employer.*

Here's an example: "Planned and managed 5K walk-a-thon fund raiser for local food bank, resulting in achieving 100 percent of food donation and cash contribution goals."

Notice the example uses two action verbs—*planned* and *managed.*

To develop worth-point "winners," start by listing three accomplishments that you are proud of.

1. ______________________________

2. ______________________________

3. ______________________________

Now, turn them into worth points by using the following formula. A good worth point uses two phrases. The first describes specifically what you did; the second, its results.

Convert your three accomplishments into worth points.

1a. What you did:

____

1b. What was the result of your action?

____

2a. What you did:

____

2b. What was the result of your action?

____

3a. What you did:

____

3b. What was the result of your action?

____

Take your time and go over your work and volunteer experience. See how many of the job actions you have listed can be "energized" by conversion into a worth point. A resume with well-written worth points literally jumps out of a stack of competing resumes!

WORTH POINT CASE STUDY

Here's another example of success that could become a worth point. During the course of the summer internship at a radio station, "Terry" is asked to reorganize a tape library, which contains previous radio spots, live broadcasts, and other recordings. During the three months onsite, she comes up with a comprehensive system to organize the spot library, using a computer database and tagging all the tapes by sponsor and air date. She put a great deal of effort and some weekend time into the project. The system was a huge hit with the traffic department and station management.

Now it's the fall semester of her senior year of college and she's drafting her resume.

Ineffective Worth Point:
Internship, Z-100 Radio, organized tape library.

That's a simple statement of an activity. Turning that into a worth point, she energizes it as follows.

Effective Worth Point:
Intern at Z-100 Radio, developed computer database system for advertising spot library resulting in 50 percent time savings to traffic and production departments.

See the difference? Terry's resume will have much more impact because she took the time to develop this worth point. First, it states she developed a functional system using a computer. Second, she had responsibility for an action. And third, Terry's actions led to a clearly stated benefit, saving the station and her employer half of the time it previously took to complete a daily task.

That's how to take an action and turn it into a worth point. If you can do that two or three times in your resume, and then remind them of those worth points in a targeted cover letter, I promise you, yours will usually be in the top 10 percent of the resumes under review.

People rarely take the time to restate what they've done action-wise with a worth point. Why? It takes time, effort, and extra thought to refine an action into a worth point. But the benefits are huge. If you haven't been in the working world very long, volunteer activities are perfectly acceptable to use as worth points.

Rev Up Your Worth Points and Resume With Action Verbs

Below is a list of action verbs to help you develop your own set of worth points.

ACTION VERB LIST

achieve
administer
affect
aid
analyze
apply
assemble
assist
attain
budget
calibrate
change
check
coach
collect
communicate
compile
compose
compute
conduct
consolidate
coordinate
create
critique
decide
demonstrate
determine
differentiate
dispense
document
earn
educate
edit
establish
evaluate
execute
expedite
facilitate
forecast
fulfill
generate
guide
hire
identify
implement
influence
initiate
illustrate
inspect
install
instruct
integrate
interpret
invent
investigate
judge
launch
lead
lecture
lobby
locate
lower
maintain
manage
measure
mentor
motivate
negotiate
operate
organize
participate
perform
persuade
plan
prepare
present
prioritize
produce
program
promote
propose
provide
publish
question
raise
recommend
record
reduce
reference
repair
replace
report
represent
research
review
rewrite
save
secure
select
sell
serve
setup
solve
speak
speed
streamline
strengthen
succeed
supervise
teach
train
translate
update
upgrade
verify
write

Action verbs are what help sell in a resume. They tell your potential employer the things you accomplished and the results that you achieved. The more assertive you are and the more confidently you can state your accomplishments and the results, the better your resume will be viewed. Sales grew, money was saved, accounts were opened, records went up the chart, or hungry people were fed. Each can be represented much more effectively as a worth point.

Don't shortchange your resume. Include worth points whenever you can and you will be amazed at the difference in the response from prospective employers. You will also find that these worth points will bring you value for a long time as they shine on your resume and cover letters. They make the case that you are a valuable asset to an employer. Remember to use them in discussions when you move on to interviews. They represent the single, most effective means to *quickly* convince your prospective boss that you are a candidate worth serious consideration. ⊙

How to Write Effective Cold and Cover Letters

What's the difference between a cold letter and a cover letter?

A "cold letter" is one that is submitted, with or without your resume, in the hopes of securing an interview with a company that interests you. A cold letter is one that you send into the unknown, often blind, as you may not know if the company is looking to hire new staff or not. Simply put, it's a shot in the dark.

A cover letter is written to address an existing opportunity at a company. Let's say you spoke to someone in the human resources department. They said, "Yes, send us a resume, here's our address." A well-written cover letter starts by referencing that this submission is being sent in response either to a specific job opening or to a company's request to review your resume and qualifications.

The cover letter accompanying your resume for a specific opportunity should also state why you believe you are qualified for the position in question. Don't assume that the resume screener will proceed far enough into your resume to the location where your carefully crafted worth points reside. Restate two or three key attributes and worth points in your cover letter, and end on a positive and enthusiastic note. Remember that the same care that went into your resume should be invested in your cover and cold letters: be sure that there are no typos, use good grammar, leave a little white space, and include your name and contact information on the letter, as it may become separated from your resume. Keep your letter to a maximum length of one page.

On the next page is a sample of a well-written cold letter I received a number of years ago. I took the time to read it and the attached resume, which looked promising. But this person never secured a phone or in-person interview with me. Why? She never took the next important step. She never made the follow-up call to see if I would give the time for an interview. Her letter said, "*I look forward to meeting with you and will be calling you in the next few weeks to arrange a mutually convenient time.*"

Dear Mr. Hatschek,

Your name came up in my research of the music business in the San Francisco region as someone whose effectiveness and influence on the industry has been exemplary. You are clearly an individual whose knowledge and experience would be invaluable to anyone hoping to enter this highly competitive and relatively closed field.

I am a musically literate, well-spoken, and enthusiastic recent college graduate whose greatest passion in life has always been music. Please be assured that I do not expect you to know of any specific positions in your or other companies. Rather, I would welcome the opportunity to meet with you briefly to discuss the business in general and get the benefit of your comments and advice.

In addition to a lifetime of collecting and listening, I have worked extensively with local acts in both promotion and staging, and am myself a singer and a songwriter. I would be happy to discuss this and other work experience in more depth when we meet.

I look forward to meeting with you and plan to call in the next few weeks to arrange a mutually convenient time.

Sincerely yours,

Jane Doe

That call never came. It may have been due to the huge number of letters she sent out, or that she landed her dream gig. But if you take the time to write a strong letter and send it out, you should budget adequate time to do at least one follow-up call for each submission.

Although I wasn't hiring at the time, I would have given this person time for an informational phone interview based on the quality of the letter and the attached resume, and that would have been a positive learning (and networking) experience for her.

Remember, often the people who have valuable information may not hire you today, but they could refer you to someone else in the industry that is hiring. So invest the time and effort to make your cold and cover letters strong, concise communicators—especially if they're aimed at what I call "Targets of Opportunity," which we will investigate in the next chapter.

A Final Thought on Originality and Accuracy in Cover Letters

I'm often asked, "Once I have one really good cover letter can I just use that as a form letter for all the jobs I respond to?" No, you must always customize each cover letter. It doesn't matter if you have thirty jobs you're responding to this week. Break it down into short-term goals for that day. Write a letter. Carefully double-check the accuracy of the spelling and the address. Pay special attention to the name of the person to whom you are sending the letter. If you are unsure of any of the contact information, call the company. "Hi, I'm sending a letter to Keith Hatschek. I just want to make sure I am spelling his last name right. Is it H-a-t-c-h-e-c-k?"

Receptionist: "No, it's got an 's' in there and no 'c' at the end."

"Oh, thank you, H-a-t-s-c-h-e-k."

You accomplished two things during that phone call. You have gotten your prospective boss's name right. And you made an impression with a person at that firm who is likely to remember that you took the time to call and find out how to spell the boss's name correctly. People remember things like that. So the cover letter originality and accuracy are very important to serious job seekers. You can and should use some of the same sentences and bullet points for similar jobs, but don't fall into the trap of sending out a generic cover letter. You're missing an opportunity to further separate yourself from the pack if you take that path. ⊙

part three

Why Most Music and Recording Industry Jobs Are Never Advertised

Tracking Down Job Openings

Do studios advertise recording engineer help wanted listings in *Billboard* or *Mix* magazine? Rarely, if at all. The reason is that they don't want to be inundated with hundreds of resumes. And of the hundreds a studio may receive if they were to advertise, how many do you think might qualify as top candidates? Perhaps a few dozen, maybe none.

There are a few exceptions, however, one being certain kinds of positions at mid- to major-sized record labels. Due to the number of employees, they're constantly re-staffing. But even those firms generally will engage an employment agency to fill many entry- and mid-level positions.

So the MRI job sleuth has a problem. If few of the jobs are advertised and each detective or sleuth is dead-set on developing a career in the music and recording industry, what should you do?

Go to an employment agency? Don't go to a local temporary services agency and say, "Hi, I really want to be an A&R assistant. Can you help me find a position?" They cannot help you. Instead, try networking, mingling with and/or joining some trade organizations. Those kinds of activities will put you on the proper trail to uncovering a wealth of unadvertised job opportunities.

Don't overlook the value of basic research in identifying job search "targets of opportunity." Let's say that in this week's issue of *Billboard* (which you stop by the library to read if you are unable to afford a subscription), you identify a company that's involved in your area of interest. Now the fun begins for a dedicated MRI detective.

As a first step in your research, you have identified a company you may want to work for. Next, you dig out the name of the hiring or personnel director by calling that company. You also soak up all the information you can about the company from the Internet. Then send your resume and a carefully crafted cover letter explaining your interest. You'll be surprised how this detective work will improve your odds of landing interviews and other potential job leads.

With each resume and cold letter submission, a good detective always asks for something in return. "I'd like to know if I might arrange an informational interview with you or so-and-so in person, or request a brief tour of your facilities." If you don't ask, you definitely won't get one. Even if they decline, the people reviewing your submission will see you are serious about your interest in their company.

What if you find out that a particular company that interests you doesn't offer informational interviews?

The next best tactic is to network with the employees. Large companies have large employee populations. A major record label has thousands of employees around the world. A large multiroom recording studio complex may have from 10 to 250 employees. They belong to trade associations, shop at local equipment dealers, and attend conventions and so forth. If you're a student in a recording program, it's likely that a recent graduate may even work there now.

Perhaps you've heard of the "six degrees of separation" concept. Each of us knows someone that is a few times removed from a target company or individual. The reality is that if you want to make a connection badly enough, you will probably uncover a means to do so. You'll strive to quench that "fire in the belly" that must be satiated with information, because as a committed MRI sleuth, you are on an information quest.

Anytime you learn of a career seminar or job fair related to your area of interest, get involved. There will be people attending from companies or labels you may want to work with or, at the very least, add to your network. Get it together and go. You have to put yourself out to get a return.

I stated that some labels do advertise entry- and mid-level positions. Pick up a copy of *Billboard* and flip to the classified section and see what jobs are listed. As I mentioned previously, most are located in New York, Los Angeles, and Nashville. There's no escaping MRI geography.

Another value of these help wanted listings is they provide the job sleuth with a barometer to measure which skills are required by today's employers. And since you'll be working on the job-specific skill set workshops for a particular career track(s), the qualifications listed in the help wanted ads let you know what skills employers are looking for in a new hire. Don't overlook this excellent guide to confirming the specific skills employers are seeking.

Your marketable skill set workshops are tools or building blocks you can use as you create your resume. Picture a job candidate walking into an interview and saying, "This is my marketable skill set." That won't work. However, it and any help wanted listing or job descriptions you locate provide you with a blueprint for your resume development. With tools such as these, and the two books by Field and SPARS referenced earlier, you can ensure that you have developed and can communicate that you have the necessary skills and attributes employers are seeking.

Here are a few examples of some help wanted listings and some decoding of the requirements listed in each.

HELP WANTED

Fast-growing, Manhattan-based distributor needs administrative assistant. Assistant to the president, experienced A/P, A/R, computer literate with letter writing ability.

That's a clerical job with some financial experience required, most likely found in a smaller company.

HELP WANTED

Assistant sales manager, telemarketer, with three years record sales experience to wholesale accounts required.

It is pretty self-explanatory. If you don't have the experience for that one, you shouldn't apply.

HELP WANTED

VP promotion, growing record company. Must have campaign experience, strong contacts with radio and press, country preferred but not necessary. No rookies.

If you don't know what campaign experience is, you'll need to find that out. Say it's January, and an artist is going to be releasing an album in April. The label is going to break the first single in March and head out on tour in May. The tour will last May through October. The many activities and promotions that are carefully combined to promote a release and the artist are combined into a campaign to benefit the label for whom that artist records. If you haven't worked on successful campaigns, this position is not for you.

Help wanted listings can help you assess the skills necessary for a particular job. They're a way for you to test your marketing skill set workshop for that position if you have one. Do the skills you think you need to do that job in the A&R department match the ones they are looking for? Because if you think it's skills A, B, and C, and three different companies are advertising for skills Q, R, and S, your marketable skill set workshop is probably incomplete or inaccurate, based on what the marketplace is seeking. In that case, regroup and develop a more accurate assessment of the marketable skill set that is required for a specific job by talking further with teachers, mentors, or working professionals in your area of interest.

Meeting the Rich and Famous

I've been asked, "Why can't I just go up and introduce myself to a top producer, engineer, or label exec and offer to work for them?" Here's why:

Every person who is already successful has a support team in place. You're better off trying to network with people whose star is on the rise, the up-and-comers who are hungry and open to making new contacts. History has proven that you are much more likely to hook up with someone on the way up than with someone already at the top. It would be difficult, if not impossible, to cold call and speak directly with a top-level artist, producer, or label honcho. They don't take anonymous phone inquiries.

In the event that you do connect with a superstar in your area of interest, it's important for you to know that many, if not all, usually have justifiable concerns about their security and privacy. It's far better if a trusted associate can introduce you. With respect to the top talent that I have had the pleasure to work with, it would be extremely intrusive to be called at home on a day off by someone that they don't know and hear, "Hey man, I love your stuff, I'd like to work for you." You will end up with a big zero for your efforts.

If you really want to connect with a top talent or executive, then find a way to be introduced by a member of their team. You want to find someone who can say, "Jim, this is somebody who really is into some of the same music we are, and I think you guys have quite a bit in common." That makes all the difference in the world. Remember one of the oldest sayings in the record business: *To get ahead, it's not just what you know, it's* ***who*** *you know.* ⊙

Schmooze or Lose
(Secrets of a Networking Guru)

The most important tactic you can use to develop key industry contacts is networking. Starting today and continuing for your entire career in the entertainment industry, commit yourself to spending a portion of each day building and nurturing your network.

Since most jobs aren't listed, it's only through networking that you uncover "hidden" opportunities. You have to consciously build and work to maintain your network. I recommend students invest two hours a week on network development. That's only fifteen minutes each day. Like other aspects of your career development, networking is *work*. If you don't hustle and sweat while you are building and maintaining your network, you won't achieve the necessary results to get ahead. The choice is yours. Net-"work," or sit back and hope your dream gig falls in your lap.

How do you manage your network? Make phone calls. Attend industry meetings, seminars, trade shows, and events whenever possible to multiply your contact with people in the business. Remember to bring your business cards.

Correspondence is an important part of your network maintenance, too.

Here's a letter I received last year.

Dear Mr. Hatschek,

I read an interesting story about your public relations firm last month in *Billboard*. I am completing my studies in studio management at XYZ University and will be visiting San Francisco this summer. I would like to see if I might stop by to introduce myself and ask for a few minutes of your time to discuss my career objectives in the music business.

Sincerely yours,

Jim O'Hara

P.S. I'll call two weeks prior to my trip, to inquire if you will be willing to make an appointment to speak with me.

Letters such as the one above will help you to get your foot in the door. The letter would have been even stronger if there was a referral included, "Joe Smith recommended I give you a call while I am San Francisco." If a professional acquaintance is willing to help make an introduction, you have a real leg-up over your competition.

Such a visit may not lead to a job offer. Maybe you're not looking for a job at this stage, especially if you are still in school. But you've just widened your network. You've got another card in your database or index file. You've got another person who knows you and you know them—your range of possibilities just increased. That's how successful networking in the entertainment business is done, day in and day out by networking gurus. With a steady investment of time, effort, and follow-up, pretty soon you'll be a networking guru too.

Networking is not a one-way enterprise. To be successful, you've got to "give" when you "get." How you do that is by being an information sponge.

For example, if you are living in L.A., there is a celebrity or charity music business event almost every weekend. You may not meet the head of each record label, but you will meet some of the staffers at those labels. One example is the TJ Martell Foundation, which was founded by members of the MRI and has been very active for twenty-five years raising funds for leukemia, cancer, and AIDS research. They regularly host charity events in L.A. and New York.

Find out when and where these and other events are being held and volunteer at a few of them. Pick up a copy of *Billboard* and find the "Good Works" listing page. Each week, you'll see a number of charity concerts, celebrity auctions, and tennis or golf tournaments, all offering an excellent opportunity to the savvy network builder to get out and start adding to their network. With the investment of a few minutes' research, a few phone calls, and perhaps a brief personal interview, you can be working with and helping out industry pros on a charitable event.

Let's say you begin with a network of twenty-five people. That's a good start. Consider them your "team." One day you make a career decision that you would prefer to work at a record label rather than a recording studio. Each person in your network may know somebody who works at a label.

Successfully working your network means that you send out an e-mail or postcard to your network stating, "Hey, I've decided to jump tracks and try to land a gig at a label, ideally one that is into hip-hop music or electronica. Do you know anyone at a label to whom you might be able to introduce me to gather more information?"

In this example, if each of the members of your network in turn has their own network of twenty-five persons, you now have a potential 625-person universe (25 x 25 = 625) in the music business to ask questions of. In this scenario, it's likely that you will get one or two positive responses to your inquiry. Your team will ask themselves, "Who do we know in the electronica and hip-hop music biz? My friend really wants to learn more about that part of the biz."

Soon you receive three e-mails back, suggesting you check out a certain label, or introducing you to a new contact at a particular company. That's networking, par excellence.

How do you go "two-way" and give back value to your network? Here's how. Let's assume that you have landed that job at a hip-hop label in L.A. One day your boss mentions that the company needs to locate a campus rep in New York City. You mention that you could send out an e-mail or postcard to your network (which, by the way, has now grown to fifty persons). Soon a number of resumes are received by fax and e-mail. Just like that, you transitioned from job seeker to job creator. That's how a person continues to grow and nurture their network.

A well-tended network should grow like a garden. It's unlikely that you will intimately know most of the people in your network. That's not important. What is important is that you manage and grow information and support those with whom you network. Doing so gives you access to an unmatched source of up-to-the-minute inside information.

At my company, Keith Hatschek & Associates, we have more than 1,000 contacts in our immediate network of associates, editors, vendors, and business acquaintances. Through them, we have the ability to communicate indirectly with another 5,000 or more people involved and interested in the industries we serve. That's a potent tool. If someone needs a photographer in Nashville, a member of our staff simply searches our database for the names and numbers of various photographers in Nashville. Sometimes we haven't met these persons personally, but they are still part our company's network. That's how the business works.

Networking represents the most surefire method to gather information about a position, industry, or company in which you have an interest. And it's the most effective means to plug into a job that's never going to be advertised. Trade associations, which we'll discuss in the next chapter, offer another important avenue to build your network.

Remember, there's a big difference between networking and interviewing. Interviews place you in a position to learn directly about a specific company or a specific job opportunity. Networking is the investment you make to meet people and share information about common career interests. Networking is the free exchange of information, usually done informally in conversation over coffee, via e-mail, or in a phone chat. You must view networking as an ongoing, constant flow of information within your network.

To excel at networking, think of it as a numbers game. Invest the time and effort to make new and different contacts. Set a goal. "I am going to network with four new people every month…" or whatever you see as being a realistic goal. Write it down, then work towards that goal and keep a scorecard to measure your progress. It is important to set and achieve short-term goals, especially with respect to growing your network.

Once you get started, you'll find it's not that hard to build up your network. Go to industry events such as seminars, open houses, and workshops that have an informational agenda. Volunteering and involving yourself in trade associations and industry organizations provides the fastest, easiest, least stressful way to expand your network resources. In San Francisco, the local chapter of the Recording Academy stages thirty-five to forty events a year. Volunteer in any capacity, even if you're making nametags and cleaning up after the event.

If you have any kind of a family or personal connection, use it. "My uncle is divorced but his ex-wife has a job in finance at Capitol Records. I'm going to see her at a wedding next month." Don't be shy. If you've got your resume ready to go, pass her a copy of it in an envelope and ask her if you can follow up to see if she might introduce you to someone in personnel. Never waste a family connection, even if you have to gather up your courage to take advantage of it.

If there's any edge you have to get a foot in the door, use it. Remember, even if that particular person is not able to assist you now, ask them who they may know that might be able to. Just because they may be family, don't expect them to treat you differently. Be professional; tell them what you can bring to the table. Explain that you are serious about a career in the business. If you are in school, explain that you are studying, learning, and networking, and are dedicated to finding a way into the music and recording business. That's critical.

Networking Statistics

It is a fact that two-thirds of MRI job seekers secure their first industry job through networking.

Never underestimate the power of networking, no matter how far up the ladder you climb. Even if you aren't the most talented individual that is pursuing your particular career path, if you are a maestro at networking, you're liable to do well.

Those of you who are musicians probably have a call file that you use for subs, musicians who have filled in for you. You've filled in for them. That's a great place to start networking.

If at first you are uncomfortable networking, don't worry. Many others have been too. Remember the definition of networking: if you are giving and getting information, and you are not a pest or a nuisance, you are successfully networking. Start with a simple introduction and alert the other person to what you are interested in. "Hi, I'm Jane and I'm looking to find a recording studio internship."

On the next page is a networking workshop to demonstrate to you that you probably have a well-developed core network. Fill it in before finishing this chapter. ⊙

WORKSHOP 7: *Networking Exercise*

Most people have approximately 250 contacts—seriously! So, take a few minutes to catalog a few of your own.

Family members

____
____
____
____
____
____

Alumni/teachers/mentors

____
____
____
____
____
____

Friends

____
____
____
____
____
____

Business contacts

____
____
____
____
____
____

Clubs/organizations

____
____
____
____
____
____

Classmates/bandmates/etc.

____
____
____
____
____
____

Digging in the Dirt
(or How I Learned to Love the Internet)

Successful job seekers hone their research and detective skills to a fine edge. And never has there been a tool with the speed, power, and access afforded by the Internet. Using the Internet as a primary research tool, students today can uncover a wealth of information in a matter of minutes. Ten years ago, putting that information together would have taken weeks or months, if it could have been located at all. Although this book doesn't provide an in-depth look at how to effectively use the Internet as a research tool, the number and quality of search engines is improving exponentially each year. So log on, type in the names of companies, career paths, or industry stars, and you'll be amazed at the wealth of information you uncover in no time at all.

What Are You Seeking?

One of my mentors said, "If you don't have dirt under your fingernails from digging to discover new things, you're never going to uncover the treasure." For job seekers, that treasure is identifying your chosen career path and embarking upon it. So be cognizant that it's up to you to do the necessary detective work to become well versed in your field of interest. Because that's the only way you will be able to compete effectively and make good career decisions when the time comes to do so.

Magazines Mirror the Industry They Cover

Today's MRI trade magazines offer a fast way to get a glimpse at the companies, trends, and trendsetters that are making news in a particular industry segment. Many of the periodicals listed in the resource section at the back of this book offer complimentary subscriptions upon request. Some are available at a newsstand. I would suggest you go and buy a copy, or investigate a good-sized public or college library to get your hands on them.

Who's hot? Who's not? What styles of music are on the way up? Which ones are on the way down? Which recording studios are hot? Which record labels are coming on strong? Magazines will tell you that. They give you the dish on the latest tools, techniques, trends, and success stories. And be sure to check out the online version of the magazines, as they will often have extended or exclusive "Web-only" content not found in the print edition.

You also have to invest time on a regular basis to mine this critical information. Set up a regular schedule. For instance, every Saturday morning, you might spend from 10 a.m. until 12 noon at a library that has a good number of industry trade magazines. Bring a roll of quarters with you.

Sit down and skim through the back issues. You'll see some articles that interest you. Photocopy them, and add these clips to your career book. Until you're working in it, reading about the business is the easiest way to learn about the industry. At the outset of your career development, this is the closest thing you have, unless you have a job, to finding out what's going on in the MRI. If you are interested in a different facet of the business, for instance, touring, artist management, radio programming, or film sound, find out what magazines cover those segments and review them religiously.

Mapping Your Career Interests

Would you try and drive cross-country without a map? Your career search requires the same kind of planning that a lengthy journey would necessitate. You've got to have a map and know a little bit about the landscape. Well, the way to begin to develop a career map and to get your bearings is to dive into the trade magazines and the Internet. The entertainment industry has embraced the Web in a big way. Most record companies have extensive Web sites that feature a wealth of information about their artists, the company, and their direction. The other fascinating part of the Internet is its global scope.

You may discover a company on the other side of the world that is involved in an area of interest that you share. And increasingly, entertainment companies are taking a global view of their business.

Our agency recently produced a professional forum. We faced a tight deadline to complete the bio for the forum's moderator. He was out of the country recording an album project and one of my colleagues was able to locate four sources with which to build a creditable bio using his discography, awards, background, and accomplishments. She accomplished this in a matter of minutes through the use of various Internet search engines. Presto! We had the bio completed in the nick of time.

If you don't have access at your home or school, call your local public library. Most libraries now offer free or low-cost Internet access.

Advanced Sleuthing

Becoming a detective is a mind-set. I've had students who have actually drawn pictures of Sherlock Holmes to place next to their computer. It graphically reminds them that one is *always* digging for information about topics and jobs of interest. Only a dedicated detective will uncover and exploit the best job opportunities.

If you'd like to be promoted from amateur detective to senior sleuth, then begin to read the bible regularly. No, not the King James version, but the "bible" of the entertainment industry segment that fascinates you. For the record industry, *Billboard* is the periodical bible.

Billboard is valuable because it tracks the pulse of the record and entertainment industry. Although it primarily covers the record business, it also covers film soundtracks, home video, recording technology, rights and publishing, copyrights, Internet, various musical genres, music distribution through the Internet, a little bit of interactive, and even reviews of industry-related books. *Billboard* gives an excellent view of the industry segments it covers.

Well before the multi-platinum *Titanic* soundtrack become one of the biggest success stories in the industry, *Billboard* had identified and tracked the relationship between hit record albums and other entertainment properties such as movies, TV shows, and video games. Recent movies such as *Austin Powers* and television shows such as *South Park* are driving hit records. Without soundtrack albums, the record business would be in trouble. Soundtrack albums such as those mentioned are keeping some record companies afloat. Those companies and executives who read and absorbed what a bible like *Billboard* reports were aware of this trend early, took advantage of it, and surfed the wave as it developed.

So identify what the bible is for the industry segments that interest you. If you're into recording technology, *Mix* and *Pro Sound News* are two of the bibles for the recording industry. For songwriting, *Performing Songwriter* is one of the best magazines. To determine your "bible," you'll need to join the right network of people working in that segment. For a songwriter, it could be a regional songwriters group or one of the performing rights societies, ASCAP, SESAC, and BMI. The people working in that segment will tell you what they rely on as their bible.

By the way, for songwriters, those performing rights organizations also produce very informative magazines for their members.

So reading your bible regularly provides a senior sleuth with up to the minute information on what's happening in the market segments they are interested in. They also often provide you with another important insight—what entry-level jobs are open and what qualifications are required.

Asking the Right Questions

Being a detective means learning to ask the right questions. Asking good questions means you must be knowledgeable before you can know exactly what to inquire about. Many people at hiring interviews have actually asked me, "Mr. Hatschek, can you tell me what you do here?"

Unfortunately, that is the kiss of death for a job seeker. I do everything I can to end that kind of interview in three minutes or less. If someone hasn't taken the time to at least find out what business occurs at the firm they're interviewing at, why should an interviewer have any interest in investing any time in them? Forget it. It's over.

Be a monster detective if you're serious about wanting to have a career in the MRI. Why? Competition. Other people are doing their detective homework. So if you don't do your research and your competition does, they're going to have a big edge when it comes time to interview and impress the future boss with their savvy and intelligence. The person who hasn't done their detective work will often appear to be just another wannabe. Few things impress a prospective employer more than an articulate job candidate who has a basic knowledge of the company's business activities. Having a few well-thought-out questions or observations to bring up in the interview is another way to make a strong positive impression. ⊙

Alphabet Soup: *All About Trade Associations*

In today's music and recording industry, there's a veritable alphabet soup of trade associations. Dozens are involved in the entertainment industry and provide excellent resources to those looking to join the business. (An appendix of some of the leading trade associations is found at the back of this book.)

It's up to you to identify, locate, and get yourself involved in these organizations on a local, regional, or national level. Most have some type of dues structure. Some offer low-cost student or trial memberships. These organizations produce newsletters, events, trade shows, and seminars, and almost every one of them has a Web site loaded with inside industry information.

What are you waiting for? Three of the most important associations for the music and recording industry, the Recording Academy (NARAS), the Audio Engineering Society (AES), and the Society of Professional Audio Recording Services (SPARS) are listed in the appendix.

These trade associations provide you with a direct link to working professionals and offer a ready-made pipeline to quickly beef up your network. As an example, in the San Francisco region there are quite a few active trade organizations: the San Francisco chapter of the Recording Academy, the student section of the Audio Engineering Society at San Francisco State University, as well as the regular AES members' section, the Northern California Songwriter's Association, the Society of Motion Picture and Television Engineers, the American Federation of Musicians (AF of M), the local chapter of the Screen Actors Guild (SAG), American Federation of Television and Radio Artists (AFTRA), and others. AF of M, SAG, and AFTRA are unions of working professionals providing additional benefits to their membership. Every one of these organizations presents an opportunity to grow your knowledge and build your network. How many exist in your region?

Most of these trade associations regularly host events and maintain a mailing list. Get on that list. Attend the events. If you can't afford the admission, see if you can volunteer in exchange for attending. Tapping into trade association resources is as easy as volunteering. If you volunteer for a trade association, you will gain information and contacts. How much easier can it be? They may not need a volunteer today, but when they do, you've got to make sure you're at the top of their volunteer list. Bring your business cards, get involved, make yourself an asset to the manager of the trade association, and before you know it, your network will be ten times its current size! But once again, you have to put in the effort to get the reward.

Some also offer job referrals, open position listings, and informal news of positions that become available. Get involved and see what types of information and resources are accessible, or you'll likely miss out on potential opportunities.

The sheer number of trade associations can be daunting—after a while they may begin to blend and look like the aforementioned alphabet soup, so pick one or two to get you started and see what develops. Remember, trade associations exist to provide information and resources to their members. Participate in them and you will move ahead much more quickly than your competitors who choose not get involved.

The last point is that these organizations provide one of the surest means, other than a personal referral, to locate working professionals who may be willing to educate and mentor you in the ways of the business. And there's no way to put a price on the value of that treasure. ⊙

Goal-Setting Skills

No matter what you tackle in life, setting and achieving goals is a key to becoming successful. And setting goals is really as simple as defining various long-term, mid-term, and short-term goals. A goal must be written down and have a date by which you will complete it. Getting a job is not a goal, because you have no control of when and if you will be hired.

As an example, let's say that your eventual goal is to become a successful songwriter. Right now you're working at a bank. But your long-term goal is to write Top-10 pop songs. You also need a mid-term goal, because it's unlikely one can go from being a bank teller to a hit songwriter overnight. So what might be a good mid-term goal? Perhaps a mid-term goal is to be a published songwriter and have two to three songs recorded on an artist's album. Pretty darn good; you got a paycheck. That's a very realistic mid-term goal.

One short-term goal is to study and learn the craft of songwriting. For instance, you discover (via detective work) that there will be a master songwriting class going on at UCLA taught by a well-known songwriter over a three-day weekend. You beg, borrow, and steal the money to go to it. Take time off work. Borrow a car if yours is a clunker. You get there because you're determined. Other short-term goals include practicing and learning your craft.

The craft of songwriting requires you to constantly be recording. At one point you'll be ready to put together a demo. You don't need to hire a symphony orchestra for your demo. If you work with one good musician-arranger, you can do just about anything that's required at this point. This demo may be a short- or mid-term goal, depending on where you start your songwriting odyssey.

How about identifying and subscribing to key trade magazines? That would be a short-term goal. Another is to locate a teacher/mentor. Say you attended a songwriting workshop given last year, and you began to correspond with one of the teachers via e-mail. Perhaps they would take on a student like yourself because you can learn so much in the right mentor or teacher relationship. Even if they're writing in a different genre than you are, the craft of songwriting is the same. And being exposed to those who are further along on your intended career path, no matter what it is, is essential to speeding up your learning process.

This is how developing your own short-, mid-, and long-term goals will help you to chart a path towards your ideal career. Let's say you identify four short-term goals and set a six-month window to complete them. Your mid-term goal mentioned above—getting songs onto a record—is your one-and-a-half- to four-year window. And your eventual goal of writing a song that goes up the charts is your five- to ten-year goal. Break it down into bite-size chunks, and you will have a clear road map to take you to your long-term goals.

Don't just stay up every night biting your fingernails worrying, trying to write that magical hit song. You may nail it, but your odds are so long it's like playing the lottery. Don't lose sight of your overall goal and timeline. Make your goals concrete with a chart in your composing room. Review the short-term activities in process *now* that are going to take you to your long-term goals.

A SONGWRITER'S ROAD TO SUCCESS

Short-term goals *6–18 months*	**Mid-term goals** *1 ½–4 years*	**Long-term goals** *5–10 years*
• Subscribe to trade magazines • Enroll in songwriting classes • Find a teacher/mentor • Join a trade association	• Publish songs • Begin building relationships with publishers, artists, managers, producers • Two to three songs recorded • Get involved in performing rights society • Investigate co-writing options • Regularly record demos, write, and pitch new material	• Record a Top-10 song • Have songs placed in films • Collaborate with leading artists and lyricists • Win Grammy for song of the year!

It's human nature to want to avoid setting goals and timelines. However, without using this tool and others like the marketable skill set workshop and the interview workshop, careers in the MRI seem distant and out of reach. You won't know if your short-term goals are in sync with what's required to make it on a particular career path if you haven't researched your area of interest. Desire alone will not make your dream a reality.

If you want to be a program director at a major market radio station, you've got to know what it takes to get there. What skills, experience, salary, and geographic moves will be required? All that information must be at your fingertips. When you have that information, it will be crystal clear to you whether or not that is the right career path for you. If you don't do your detective work, you may spend months or years pursuing a career path that really isn't what you want from life. Don't make that mistake.

That's why goal setting is so important in this industry, because everybody is following their star and chasing their dream. Almost everyone wants to write, record, sing, or engineer that smash hit. But how do you put yourself in the situation where you're actually working with the artist who can write those hit songs? How can you work with a Tony Brown, Glen Ballard, or Quincy Jones?

Defining and achieving the little steps (short- and mid-term goals) will help you achieve your long-term goals.

So to recap, you need to identify attainable goals and set a timeline for accomplishing each one. Review goals as often as possible. Use the two one-year calendars in your career book to track your progress. Update your goals as you move forward. Some will be completed and you can cross them off. New ones will become clear to you as you continue your career development.

Finally, remember to be patient. Maintain and update your goals, pat yourself on the back when you accomplish each one, and let the goal-setting process work for you. If you are diligent in maintaining your goals, you have a much better chance of achieving long-term success. ⊙

Preparing for Interview Success

The Value of Informational Interviews

Informational interviews help you gather information on a company or a position without being in the potentially stressful situation of an actual hiring interview.

Before we look at how you can secure an informational interview and then craft the questions that will elicit the most useful information, remember that in today's increasingly hectic working world, people often will not or cannot make time for such activities. Don't be dismayed if your requests for informational interviews result in turndowns most of the time. Sooner or later you will land a few. Only then will you discover the wealth of information that such an interview can bring to your job search.

In terms of landing an appointment for such an informational interview, a referral from a member of your network is the most reliable means to secure one. The second most reliable method is to connect with a working professional at a conference, trade show, or through a trade association. That's another reason why you need to be in the flow of the market sector that interests you, whether you have a job or not. If you are hidden at home, you can't very well meet those persons who can help you.

If you will be approaching a company or person "cold" for such an interview, here's the most effective approach.

Introduce yourself via letter, phone, or e-mail. Explain briefly who you are and why you are getting in touch. Ideally, you will have the name of the person with whom you would like to meet. They may be the studio manager, head of personnel, or tour manager. Be sure that you are professional and polite, enlisting the help of the person answering the phone in getting an "at bat" to request an informational interview. Do not antagonize the receptionist or assistant, also known as the screener. If they have to put you on hold, let them know that it's "no problem" for you to wait until they can get back on the line.

If you actually are connected with the person you wish to meet—or their assistant—once again be clear about who you are and why you are calling. Now is the time to clearly state that you are asking for a brief appointment (fifteen minutes is a good length) to find out a bit more about the industry and the company. If they say no, then remember to ask if there is another person in the company who might be able to share a few minutes, either in person or by phone. Another option is that the person to whom you are speaking may know of another working professional they believe may be helpful for you to contact. Always end with a polite thank-you for each person's time, no matter what the outcome is.

Once you land an informational interview, there is a workshop on the next page with some of the basic questions to ask. If you are so inclined, take along a pocket tape recorder and ask if you can tape the interview. If you or the interview subject is not comfortable with a recording, then at least take a pocket note pad and jot down their key comments.

The speed at which valuable information will be coming at you during such an interview will make taking notes a necessity. You won't have the luxury of calling them back to check a fact, name, or phone number. Take your time, and when an important point is made, repeat that point aloud to confirm that you understood exactly what they are saying.

WORKSHOP 8:
Informational Interview Guidelines

You're in your interview… now what? After outlining briefly—in one or two sentences—why you are there and your career goals, use this list of questions as a guide. Be sure to start the interview by asking how much time your interview subject is able to share with you. Then stick to that timetable.

1. ***What do you look for when you are hiring a ________________ ?*** *(Fill in the job you are researching.)*

2. ***Will I need special training or education?***

3. ***If so, where is the best place to get such training?***

4. ***Is specific job experience required? If so, what kind? More importantly, how would you recommend getting such experience?***

5. ***Is there any way to break into this field without on-the-job experience?***

6. ***These are the skills and abilities I have developed.*** *(Briefly outline your basic skills and/or hand over your carefully crafted resume.)* ***What do you think my chances are of being hired as a____________ ?***

7. ***Do you have any suggestions for me to increase my chances for being hired as a____________?***

8. ***Do you hire people in this capacity often? What's the supply-and-demand situation in terms of job seekers and available jobs in this field?***

9. ***To what level can a person hired at the entry level advance?***

10. ***What is the usual starting salary? After two years?***

11. ***Does your company offer internships?***

12. ***Can you suggest other companies or people to contact?***

13. ***What is the most important attribute that someone wishing to enter the field today should possess?***

This list will result in a lengthy interview if all the questions are discussed. If time is tight, you will have to prioritize these questions for each informational interview you secure.

Your informational interview subjects will pass on a wealth of information in the short time that you are with each of them. Their answers will serve as a road map to fine-tune your career development and job search.

It's only going to take two or three productive informational interviews to understand exactly which skills are requirements for success for a given job and whether or not you are currently employable in a particular position.

Are such informational interviews easy to obtain? No. Why? Everybody has twelve hours of work to do in nine hours. How are they going to get it done? Many executives and middle managers are just too busy to even consider such interviews. That's why nurturing your network to get an introduction when you are ready for it is so vital to your career development.

If you can't approach a person or a company directly, you may connect with them at a professional meeting, seminar, conference, lecture, or class. In that setting, professionals will often say, "I loved speaking to the class today, so here is my e-mail address if you have any other questions." If you don't write that down and send them an e-mail, you are squandering a prime opportunity.

Every time you have an opportunity to network with a working professional, you should take it regardless of whether or not that person is directly on the career path you see yourself taking today. You never know when having a wider network may help you. You've got to have access to fresh, reliable industry information to make the most of your career opportunities. In addition to what you will learn from magazines, books, seminars, and classes, networking provides the best source of locally relevant information for someone on a career search.

What else do you bring to your informational interview? Two resumes and some business cards. When you get home from that informational interview, promptly write a thank-you note. Thank them for their time and the information they shared.

The Job Interview

Let's assume you've submitted a resume for a position that is advertised or that you've learned about through your network, and you've been called in for an interview. How do you maximize this opportunity?

On the next page is a checklist of what you should do in advance to prepare for the interview.

PRE-INTERVIEW CHECKLIST

	YES	NO
1. Your resume is in tip-top shape.	☐	☐
2. You know something about the company and, if possible, the person with whom you will be meeting.	☐	☐
3. You have a handful of your business cards.	☐	☐
4. You have practiced the interview workshop on the following pages with a friend or family member. If the interview is for a particular job opening, use the list on page 93–94. If it is an informational interview, use the list on page 89.	☐	☐
5. Dress neatly and present yourself professionally.	☐	☐
6. Plan to arrive a few minutes early, especially if you are traveling there for the first time.	☐	☐
7. Jot down a few questions about the company, its activities, and the requirements for an employee's success in that company. Make a note to ask these questions during your interview.	☐	☐
8. Bring a note pad and pen.	☐	☐

During the interview itself, just concentrate on being yourself and answering questions as directly and honestly as you can. If you are at the entry-level stage of your career, the person interviewing you doesn't expect you to have all the answers. What they *are* looking for is intelligence, a positive attitude, and whether or not they feel there will be a fit between you and the company.

Take the time to look around the company offices and take a few mental notes. Are the offices neat, bright, and pleasant? Do the people working there smile and address you directly? Is this the kind of place you would like to come to each day? If not, no matter how good an offer, you should consider these factors. Also, if there are pictures of sailboats in the office of your interviewer, and you happen to have a family member who sails, take the initiative to mention that point and use it to build a rapport.

How should you dress for an interview? Dress appropriately for the company. Determine appropriate dress by doing your homework. If you're going for an interview to a company that does concert production and sound reinforcement, their stock in trade is building, moving, and maintaining big, heavy pieces of equipment. You definitely don't want to be wearing an Armani suit. However, if you're wearing a pair of khaki pants and a neatly pressed shirt with a collar, you will look professional and neat. If you are interviewing at a well-known Madison Avenue entertainment law firm, you would wear a suit. The impression you make with your dress, your manner, and your questions and comments set you apart—to your benefit or your detriment. The choice is yours to make. So take the time to rehearse carefully so you are as comfortable and confident as possible.

Now let's look at the interview drill workshop on the next pages. It will allow you to build your confidence by practicing aloud the types of questions that you are likely to be asked during an actual job interview.

It's important to spend some time thinking about and writing down your answers to these types of questions. Equally important is practicing the interview drills out loud with a friend or family member. Do it more than once. The more familiar you are talking about yourself, your qualifications, and your worth points (how you have created value for your employer in the past), the better the impression. Be prepared to the point that discussing your interests and skills is second nature. Doing so will give you the confidence to present yourself at your best.

WORKSHOP 9:
Develop Your Interviewing Skills

You wouldn't show up for a gig with your band without adequate rehearsal, would you? Don't shortchange yourself in an interview. Rehearsal will allow you to be at your best.

Start by looking carefully at the questions below, and write down your answers. You will have to do some thinking. Don't expect to draft perfect answers on the first attempt. Interviews can be tense for all parties, and practicing will build your confidence! Once you have answers that you feel comfortable with, it's time to enlist the help of a friend or family member to drill you and strengthen your interview skills.

Job Interview Practice Session

The interviewer is Dana Carlton, Human Resources Coordinator for IRS Records, Santa Monica, CA. The interviewee is you.

Questions

1. ***How did you learn about our company?***
2. ***What do you feel qualifies you to work at IRS Records?***
3. ***In your past work experience, what have you enjoyed doing the most?***
4. ***What part of your working experience was least enjoyable?***
5. ***Where do you see your career taking you over the next two to four years?***
6. ***If we don't have any openings for paid positions at this time would you consider an unpaid internship?***
7. ***Any other skills or accomplishments that you would like to share with me before we finish up today?***

Interviewee: Remember to always thank your interviewer for the time they have spent talking with you. Time is the most precious commodity any busy professional can share.

Use this workshop again as a review before you go out on an actual job interview. Answer questions in an even pace, and take a minute to think about your answers. Above all, if you don't know the answer to a specific question on an actual interview (especially if it is a technical question), don't be afraid to answer by saying, "I don't know the answer, but I'm sure I could find out."

How is your body language? Try not to be tense and nervous, and remember to speak clearly. It is important to show enthusiasm and make eye contact with your interviewer.

Remember that any interview is, first and foremost, your best opportunity to make a positive impression on a potential employer or a referral to employment. Make the most of each interview by being well prepared and ready to answer basic questions such as these. If possible, secure the full name and accurate pronunciation of your interviewer's name in advance. Bring at least two copies of your current resume, and have some current information about the company so you can show you have done some research.

Review these questions and practice your answers aloud at least three times before going on any interview. Do your homework before you step into that office, and your interviews will bring a handsome reward!

The questions in the interview practice session are similar to those that you're likely to be asked if you're actually applying for a job. If you don't practice answering them, odds are that you may say something that you regret.

If an interviewer asks, "What do you think qualifies you to work at XYZ record label?" be ready to answer that with some of your worth points. Do your preparation on the company in advance. Know something about what they do and mention what you know about the company and their business in the interview. Before you go on the interview, practice stating your worth points and the information you have dug out about the company. Speaking in front of a mirror or with a friend makes all of the difference.

In addition to your enthusiasm, experience, and qualifications, which should be evident from your personal demeanor as well as your well-crafted resume, your interviewer is trying to determine, "Will they work hard, do they know a bit about the business, do they seem stable and trustworthy?" On the business side of the industry, your presentation will be more important. Do you look professional? Do you sound articulate? Do you have communication skills? Are you adept on the phone? Your interviewer may say, "Bill, come to my desk and pick up the phone. We want to ask you a few questions over the phone." Or they may ask you to sit down and take an aptitude test to measure your ability to follow directions, do simple math, and assess your command of the written word. Be ready.

Practice makes perfect, so don't shortchange yourself by going into an interview unprepared. Be prepared for informational interviews as well, because you never know when an informational interview may turn into a job interview. ⊙

Internships: Learn Before You Earn

Internships can offer an effective bridge to a job in the music and recording industry. A good internship position puts you in a working environment where professionals are practicing their craft in your specific field of interest.

Although I am a strong proponent of internships since they provide an unparalleled real-world learning experience, they also may tax your financial health: Many MRI internships are unpaid positions. A few paid internships do exist and they are competed for fiercely. However, even an unpaid internship can be extremely valuable to your career development if you plan for it properly and set a goal for what you can learn.

To get the most from an internship, expose yourself to as many facets of the company's operations as possible. Avoid no task or activity that can help you grow. If you see the company president is hosting a golf tournament, volunteer to help. The more you can rub elbows with the movers and the shakers, the more benefit you will receive from your internship.

Learning how to set up a tape recorder, mail out a press release, or wind a cable properly isn't the only thing you want to master. Many benefits accrue for savvy interns who network with the employees they meet.

Another way to maximize the benefits from an internship is to widen your exposure at the company. As an example, if you intern three days a week at a record label, perhaps you could come in one of the other days and be a shadow in another department. That way you will learn more about what's done in the legal department, the art department, or the promotions department.

My bottom line on internships is that they provide outstanding opportunities for a person who wants to learn and get established in the industry. But there are exceptions, situations where a few companies may take unfair advantage of so-called "interns" to get free labor, with little or no learning or mentoring offered in the exchange. I've known interns who were faced with requests for unpaid activities that, frankly, were way above and beyond the call of duty for what amounts to a

volunteer position. My advice to those facing such a situation is to use common sense in judging whether or not you should commit to
a seemingly inappropriate or overwhelming task.

If you find yourself in what appears to be an abusive internship situation, paid or unpaid, bring that to the attention of the supervisor or boss. State your concern calmly and listen carefully to their response. What's the worst thing that might happen? They may let you go. If that does happen, don't fret. You probably aren't going to have a career at a firm that does not value every member of its team, even a "lowly" intern.

A few unscrupulous employers may take advantage of an intern if they can. Should you be wary of all internships? Absolutely not. There are many fabulous internships. If you are enrolled in a school program in music or the recording arts, you likely have access to internships that have been tested by previous students and recommended by faculty. This is a good approach to landing the right internship that can be your stepping stone to your first job offer.

One studio manager at a leading world-class recording facility candidly remarked to me that "the first place we look to fill an opening is our pool of current and past interns. They know our business and what we expect in an employee."

On the Job/Your Internship

Once you arrive at your internship, a new level of learning begins. Although academic training is important, there's only so much you're going to learn in a classroom environment. When you've got an artist breathing down your neck demanding, "Where's the guitar track that I just played?" your motivation to learn quickly is definitely heightened. When you're in a classroom environment, there is a different dynamic. When a client is paying $300 per hour to be in a studio and they're not happy, it changes the landscape and your priorities significantly.

What will make you, as an intern, valuable to your future boss? That's the golden question that interns perennially seek to answer. Here are the key attributes that employers look for most when hiring.

MRI EMPLOYER'S WISH LIST

1. **Problem-solving ability** is very important. Bosses generally are bosses because they're the best at dealing with a million and one problems. So if you develop problem-solving skills, chances are you're going to go a long way toward impressing your supervisor.

2. **Technical skills** also play a part, too—especially if you've charted a career path on a technical track.

3. The ability to **responsibly complete assignments** is a critical skill. Employees who can work effectively in a self-directed manner are a big asset.

4. There are not "white-coated operators" standing by at every recording studio and record label waiting for job assignments. There are just enough people to get by and sometimes not quite enough people to get by. So to succeed in this industry you're going to have to **hustle**. You'll have to work some weekends. You will occasionally stay until midnight to complete an important job. It's the nature of the beast. The entertainment industry is not like the retail business, in which shops are open from 10 a.m. to 6 p.m. and then everyone heads home. Weekends? Prepare to sacrifice quite a few of them over the course of your career.

5. **Perseverance** keeps turning up as another key attribute. Early in my career, a publisher told me, "Keith, you've got to be in the right place at the right time… and that means being aware of what's going on in all the areas you have an interest, all the time."

   What he meant is that if you're serious about a career in the MRI, you have to get plugged in so that you have constant access to the information that relates to your interests. You have to be ready to network every minute of every day, even if you've got a nonmusic job. You may be pleasantly surprised to discover that someone in the company at which you work has a kid or a nephew or an uncle who works at a label or a studio. Let people know what your aspirations are.

   Not to the point of annoyance, but it's good to voice where you are headed in the long run to those you feel close to at your day job. "I enjoy working here, but I'm also writing songs every chance I get and studying how to become a successful songwriter." You never know where you're going to make a key connection.

6. **Integrity** is a key component of your success, not only as an intern, but all the way to the top. When you say you're going to do something, do it. If you say you're going to do something and you realize you can't, don't be afraid to go back and say, "You know, I really can't do that." People will respect you for that far more than if you hide under a blanket and think, "I hope they forgot I said I was going to do that."

   Your boss and coworkers are not likely to forget your failure to live up to your promise to perform. The entertainment industry is surprisingly small and most people have good memories. It's okay to regroup and say you can't deliver, but it is a huge liability to just blow off an assignment, no matter how trivial it may seem to you.

Financial Survival for Interns

The last concern prospective interns have is usually the biggest one: that is, the lack of pay from the employer even though, as an intern, you must make a firm commitment of time, effort, and energy. If a studio calls up and offers an internship and it doesn't pay, you may have to do a little finagling, especially if you have a full time "day gig" to pay your bills. You may have to ask the boss at your day gig if you could work flexible hours for six months. That's why it's helpful to let people know a little about your long-term quest to be successful in the music industry. Most people want to see others succeed in the long run.

The worst thing that can happen is that your day job boss will say, "No!" and you'll have to choose to decline the internship or look for another day gig.

The key thing with internships is to try to land an internship that is managed, in which they can say to you, "Here's what our internship offers you." That's important. Because if your internship description consists of "clean up and setup, make coffee, and clean the bathrooms," you might want to look around a little more. Ask a few more questions, because a successful internship is a two-way street—a give-and-get proposition.

A good internship program should offer you learning opportunities, and you should be interviewing the intern managers as much as they are interviewing you. "Mr. Studio Manager, if I intern at your studio, would there be some learning opportunities for me? What would they include?" If you get a good answer to that, it's a very positive sign. However, if you don't, or if they hem and haw a bit, that's a warning sign.

Find out if there will be an opportunity to ask questions of the senior staff at some point. If they don't have an answer to that question, you've got a problem. If you have to do any errands or traveling, will you be reimbursed for gas? It's smart to ask those kinds of questions up front.

A few internships, usually with the larger companies such as record labels, actually offer minimum wage to interns, as they understand the mutual benefit of actually offering a paycheck, however small.

Why is that? The intern, even when receiving a small paycheck, is often more committed. And the employer, since they are actually paying, thinks, "It's a resource, we're paying for it," instead of saying, "She's an intern, she sits and reads *Billboard* for four hours and only does fifteen minutes of work." So ask questions and if possible, speak with a current or past intern to hear what they learned during their internship.

Another key is to network with your friends and acquaintances. Let your friends who have similar interests know: "I did an internship at such and such company and they're looking for more people now!" If you're in a school program, network with other students constantly.

I really believe in the value of internships. However, try to find one where you really believe you've got an opportunity to learn. Prepare yourself, since you may need to work a part-time job or save up enough money to focus on your internship. Earning will come later in your career. Do not mistake your internship as an earning opportunity. It is a way to enhance your "hireability" as soon as you absorb what knowledge you can.

Remember, an internship is temporary. Go into an internship knowing that it is not your permanent station in life. Secondly, in a good internship, there's a balance between learning and earning: earning for the company and the boss, and learning what they do to enhance your marketable skill set.

Not all internships lead to your next step on that career ladder. A former student called to say, "Oh-h-h-h, that internship was a nightmare. I had no idea what a MRI public relations firm did. I was licking envelopes and running a copy machine in a tiny, hot room. I was sorting hundreds of pieces of mail and clipping articles with an X-acto knife. I was there until 2 a.m. because there was an ad campaign breaking, and we had to assemble and hand out goodie bags to 10,000 people at an event at 6 a.m. the next morning. After three months, I knew I had to quit."

Guess what? That was the *second* most valuable internship that person could have had at that point. Why? Because they now know for sure that they are not cut out to work in entertainment public relations. The *most* valuable internship is one that leads to a job offer in your area of interest. ⦿

part four

Preparing for Your Job Search

Let's assume that you have at least one marketing skill set workshop completed. You've got a career path and a ladder that you've investigated and that interests you. You've done a bit of research on the job, divining the earning potential from grunt to big cheese on your chosen career path...you even have a plan to survive financially while you establish yourself and get your foot in the door with an unpaid internship. In this chapter, I'll provide advice that will help you to get the greatest results from your forthcoming job search efforts.

Your Attitude Will Determine Your Altitude

I can't overemphasize the importance of bringing a positive attitude to your job and to your job search. Why? Because no one wants to be around folks that are grumpy or out of sorts. Work is tough, full of stress and challenges. You have to be able to come in and say, *"Okay, how can I contribute? How do I create value for the company? How do I make my bosses more successful?"*

That's really what you should be thinking about when you're heading into an interview or a potential job situation: *What are you capable of doing to make that company measurably better?*

And when it does come to an interview for a prospective internship or job, having a positive attitude will make it easier for you to communicate what you've done elsewhere in the past. Even if you haven't had any big career successes yet, be sure to notice the noteworthy accomplishments on your resume. You can work at a local level. Volunteer at a local organization. Any place where you personally make a change is a notch in your career belt, and that's the information that you need to present clearly in a job interview. Having a positive attitude goes a long way in making the impression that you are someone that would be valuable to an organization.

Investment in Your Search

You're going to have to invest a bit of cash in your job search. I briefly mentioned the Internet as a resource. Once again I am continually amazed when I'll ask, "I wonder what this company does?" And I'll tap, tap, tap, tap, tap on my computer keyboard until the information comes on to my screen. But, by and large, the information is out there if you're willing to look for it.

For those of you who aspire to be songwriters, you need to get yourself on the mailing list of every songwriter's organization there is, local, national, and international. Learn about performing rights societies and how they can help your career. (The leading performing rights societies are ASCAP and BMI. They are listed in the appendix of trade organizations at the back of this book.)

If you want to be a recording engineer or producer, you should become a member of the Recording Academy (NARAS). Learn about SPARS and the AES, organizations that serve the recording studio, engineer, and producer community. (These are also listed in the same appendix referenced above.)

If you want a career in broadcasting, you've got to seek out similar associations. You should find out about **E3 (Electronic Entertainment Expo)** and their annual trade show featuring the latest in interactive entertainment, connections to trade associations, the **Computer Games Developer's Conference**, and other similar events. Get involved. It's vitally important to continually meet people and learn. Invest the time and membership dues to participate in a pertinent trade organization that is on the career path that interests you.

Tools and Information Resources

What are the basic tools you're going to need to do your job search?

First, your resume. You'll need that soon enough, but not in the research phase.

How do you learn about companies? Start by utilizing the tools that everyone has access to: the telephone and the Internet. Another great source of information about companies, jobs, and entertainment industry career paths are the books and trade magazines available in many libraries.

Many books are updated every four to five years. In terms of the freshness of the information, they are not as current as a trade magazine or the Internet. Trade magazines provide fresh information monthly or weekly, depending on their publication schedule.

The Internet provides access to information that is often updated daily. Each day you can log onto a major label's Web site to find out what's going on that day. Even if the label Web site is primarily aimed at consumers, record buyers, and fans, there's usually other information about the label to be found on the site. Smaller, independent labels often post job listings online.

What else will you need to invest in your career development? Time. You need to make a commitment to set up a time budget. When you first moved out of your parents' house, you had to figure out what you could spend on rent, car insurance, food, clothing, etc. In the same way, you need to set up a time budget to succeed in your job search.

Can you afford to spend ten hours a week? Can you afford to spend two hours a week? Once you have a time budget, keep a log of your time. For example, on November 15, I invested one hour. The most important aspect of your career development time budget is to be consistent and stick with it every week, be it ten hours or one.

Many trade magazines such as *Billboard*, *Mix*, *Radio and Records*, and *Variety* are now online. *Billboard* is partially online. In my opinion there's still no substitute for the actual magazine. You see the pictures, read editorials, plus many trade magazines have reader response cards, nicknamed "bingo cards," allowing readers to request free literature from advertisers.

Another place to mine information is company literature. If the company is publicly traded, you can locate their 10K statement. This lists the officers of the company, what state are they headquartered in, how many employees they have, and their annual report. You may also find much of that information on their Web site.

I also recommend some basic tools because they have proven to be effective for me. I have a Rolodex™ and card file. If you don't want to spend the $20 for a Rolodex, you can simply buy a card file. By a card file, I mean one of those little boxes you can buy at a drug store for $1.99, as pictured below. It's plastic, rectangular, and holds about 150 3"x 5" or 4" x 6" cards. It's a fabulous (and inexpensive) way to keep your assets and your information resources organized. Another alternative is a Filofax™ organizer.

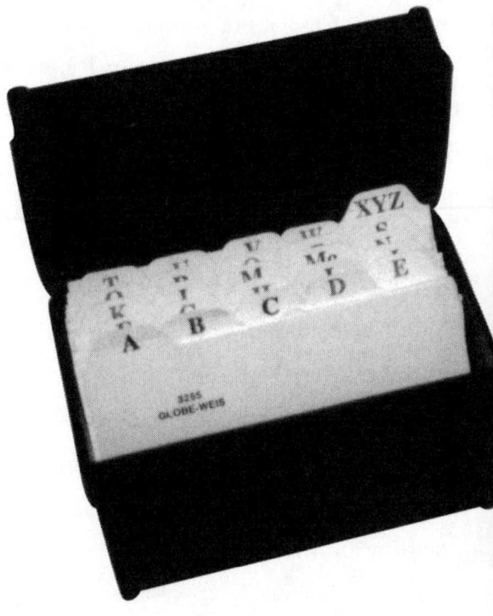

You also may consider purchasing a sheet business card holder, above.

When you get a new contact's business card, staple it onto a 3" x 5" card. File it in the box in alphabetical order using a set of tabbed card dividers sized for the card file. If you do an interview, make some notes about what you discussed or learned. Be sure to write down the name of the receptionist or the secretary of the company that you interviewed at on that same 3" x 5" card. Then, if you go for a second interview, you've got that card, and you can bring it with you. You can know that the receptionist's name is Mary or Jim, and you will make an impression that you are sharp and personable. That impression is crucial to separate you from the other interviewees.

You may also get a special business card holder such as the one pictured, right. The most basic ones hold up to sixty cards and can be bought for less than $5 at an office supply store.

If you want to go a bit more high tech, for about $25 you can get an electronic organizer to store phone and fax numbers, and e-mail addresses. You can take this with you when you're on the go. More sophisticated portable digital assistants, such as those from Palm, Handspring, and Sony, offer expanded functions including e-mail, at a proportionately greater cost.

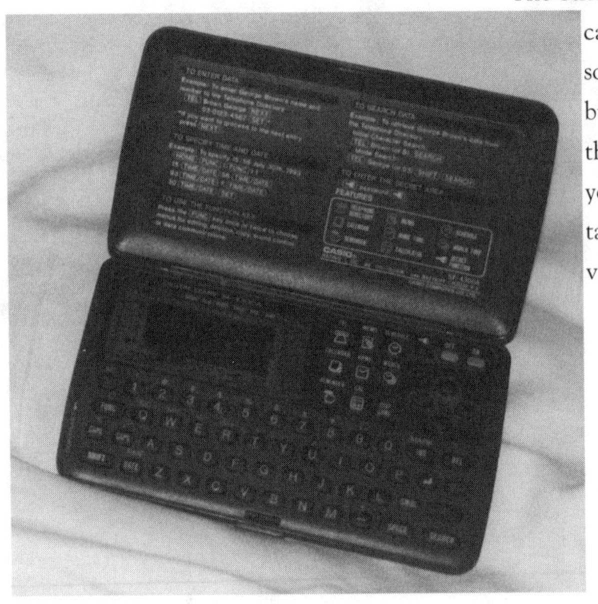

Your own business cards are a must. I strongly encourage you to invest in them as soon as you're ready to begin your job search. Office supply stores such as Office Depot, Office Max, or Staples can design and print 500 simple business cards for less than $20.

Business cards are something job seekers often overlook. Have them made even if you don't have a job or internship yet. They set a professional tone with anyone you interact with. Even if you are working a day gig, you don't have to list your day gig on your business card. It can just include your name, address, and contact information.

The other benefit to having a business card is that when you meet someone, you give that person a business card. Most of the time, they will pass their card back to you, so you have another contact to add to your growing universe of industry contacts. ⊙

Are You Ready to Hit the Streets?

If you've done your detective work, performed the workshops outlined earlier in this book, developed a rock-solid resume, and started to build your network of contacts, then you're probably itching to hit the streets and put your new career-building skills to work.

As you head out the door or to your telephone, here are a few key attributes that will help you to accomplish your goals.

- **Enthusiasm** is essential to making a favorable impression on your future boss and co-workers. I underlined the last four letters of this word. Those four letters, "IASM," stand for "I Am Sold Myself." It's hard to convince your future boss that you're the best person to hire if you don't display confidence in yourself. Building confidence requires you to practice communicating effectively with those in the industry.
- None of you who play a musical instrument would want to appear in front of an audience without a **rehearsal**. Likewise, if you're going to an interview, whether it's informational or a final interview for the job of your dreams, don't do it without first practicing. Chapter 18 provides a blueprint to develop your basic interviewing skills. Rehearsing your interview will give you confidence. That confidence will translate into enthusiasm and the ability to communicate your skills, attributes, and career goals to those you meet, whether it's at an industry event or an interview. This will make a tremendous difference in the quality of your interview experience. Critique your practice interviews.
- What else will help you build your confidence? Start with a good resume. Regularly practice your interviewing skills. Dig up information on the company with which you have an interview or tour arranged. Be ready with well-prepared questions. Succeeding in your career search requires you to be enthusiastic, knowledgeable, practiced, and confident. The way to accomplish that is **adequate preparation**.
- The next key to getting that job is to clearly communicate the **results** of what you've accomplished so far in your working history. In sales terms, that means you need to highlight the "benefits" and not the "features." Here's an example of the difference between features and benefits.

Say you live in Palm Springs or Orlando. Every car should be equipped with air conditioning in such hot climates. If I'm a car salesman and I say to a prospective buyer, "This car has air conditioning, it's really nice," I've merely told a prospective buyer about the A/C feature. I'll be much more successful in getting my customer to want that air conditioner if I communicate, "Remember last week when the temperature reached 102 degrees? This nicely air-conditioned car will keep you cool and comfortable, no matter what the weather is like." The comfort that the buyer will experience illustrates the benefit they will get if they purchase an auto with A/C.

Think of yourself in terms of the benefits you can create for your prospective employer. Can you make their life easier, more profitable, and more comfortable? If so, how? Will they have more free time because of your competency? Can you increase their bottom line because of what you can do for them? You must communicate the benefits that they will obtain if they hire you.

There's no better way to accomplish this than by stating your worth points in your resume, your cover letter, and most importantly, in person during your interview. Skip back to chapter 11 and read your sample worth points out loud. They clearly state the benefits you created in a no-nonsense manner.

Be careful not to overstate or overhype your accomplishments. No employer wants an overblown, narcissistic employee on his or her staff. But if you state your worth points and demonstrate how you can contribute to the company, you will have made a favorable impression, one that is likely to land you in the top tier of candidates for the job you seek. To convince them, you must demonstrate you are the *best* person for the job.

- Another key action after you've completed an interview is to **follow-up** in writing. Re-emphasize the key benefits you believe you can contribute if hired. At some point during your interview, take a moment to ask your interviewer the following question, "I appreciate the time you've spent telling me more about the company and what kinds of job opportunities exist here. Could you identify what are the two or three key attributes it will take for a person to be successful at this job (or in this company)?"

Listen very carefully to their reply and make a note of what they say. Then, you can write a thank-you note to your interviewer. (You did remember to ask for a business card, so you are sure to use the correct spelling of their name and title, didn't you?) Now, you're in a position to not only thank them for the interview, which demonstrates your professionalism, but you can also briefly restate how your marketable skill set will make you an asset to the company. If it's a specific position that you are interviewing for, you can state that your skills, worth points, enthusiasm, and experience would be an excellent fit with the company… based on what you learned during your interview.

It's your responsibility to communicate with your prospective employer why you are the best choice. Employers will rarely read between the lines on your resume and cover letter. They don't have the time. However, if you've done your homework and arrive prepared with many of the things outlined in this book, your prospective employer is likely to think, "This person seems articulate, informed, and has relevant job experience. They also took the time to find a little bit of information about us." When you hit them with a follow-up letter that restates your experience and your sincere interest, you score a few more points.

Should you follow up by e-mail? I suggest you use paper because generally if you're still in the running for a position, the company is likely to add your follow-up note to your file. If it's e-mail, they may not print it out. Also, I believe that e-mail is still a bit ephemeral in today's businessworld. Always save a copy of your follow-up correspondence.

- As your career develops, it's important to demonstrate your **progressive career growth.** That is, how you have increased your skills, your responsibility, and the value you created for your employers over time.

For instance, if you are climbing the technical track of the studio career ladder covered in chapter 5, you probably started off sweeping floors, running errands, and making coffee as a gofer. Then you moved up to making tape copies and soon were assisting on sessions, setting up the tape machines and microphones in the studio. That's progressive career growth. It shows your progress and represents a very powerful method to sell you to your next boss as someone on the way up. You've missed a very important opportunity if all you communicate on your resume is that you "worked in a recording studio."

Progressive career growth shows a prospective employer that you've evolved. That's one of the career keys your next boss really wants to see. Over time, you will develop from a one-page to a one-and-a-half-page resume. You will be able to communicate verbally and in writing the way that you have developed and the specific areas where you have created benefits (don't forget those!) on your previous gig. Use as many action verbs as you are able. Employers are much more likely to hire someone who is able to demonstrate they are on the way up.

- Sell yourself by showing the **solutions** you've developed in the past. Once again, I cannot overemphasize the importance of investing the time to develop the worth points that were covered in chapter 11.

  Show a prospective employer the benefit of your actions, not just the action you took. This is the single, most powerful attribute you can communicate as you search for your job.

Keep these four tips in mind:

1. Bring enthusiasm.
2. Communicate the measurable benefits previous employers enjoyed due to your efforts.
3. Follow up religiously.
4. As your career develops, highlight your progressive career growth.

Doing these four things now and throughout your working life in the entertainment business will help you get to the head of the class as you develop your career.

Make Time for One Last Money, Geography, and Gut Check

At this point in your MRI career game plan, I recommend you conduct one more "reality check." Based on correspondence with some of my former students, there are three important factors that you should check about the specific job you have targeted.

Salary: Is there the potential to earn the kind of salary you need both to survive in the short term and to prosper in the long term? Remember the earning range on the technical career track in the recording studio? It may take a person two to three years or longer to make it to the role of a first engineer. Ask yourself if you are willing to work and sacrifice at the salaries you have researched to make the climb up the ladder.

Geography: If your family or best friends are all in your hometown, are you ready to move on to one of the major urban centers where the entertainment business is percolating? Prepare for new surroundings, new stimuli, and if you are moving to New York or Los Angeles, a significantly higher cost of living. Are you willing to make the move? To succeed as a songwriter, many move to Nashville at some point in their career.

If you want to flourish as a recording engineer for film, television, or post production, you likely will be in L.A. or New York, and maybe even London. If you have deep roots in your hometown or perhaps your wife or husband has a solid career there, now is the time to really consider the "G" for geography factor. Are you willing to spread your wings and move?

Use the Internet to gauge the cost of living in the various cities or regions you are investigating. Since the cost of a similar apartment can vary by a factor of ten times from Manhattan to Austin, you need to do the same kind of research on the prospective cost of living that you performed on the various career paths that interested you. Put those detective and Internet research skills to work. Don't forget possible higher car insurance premiums, parking, and other costs unique to a big city environment, if that's where your career path seems to be headed.

Gut Check: Have you prepared yourself for the rejection involved in working your way into the MRI business? There are tens of thousands of persons seeking employment in the entertainment industry, and that competition makes it easy for prospective employers to sometimes treat those who are seeking a job with little or no respect. Unfortunately, it's probable that you will have the door slammed in your face, literally or figuratively, many times in the course of your job search.

Get yourself ready for it. You will experience negativity. You'll have people tell you (as they did me), "Why pursue this career? You'll never make any money," or the ever-popular, "Why don't you get a *real* job?"

If you don't have a burning desire, that fire in the belly, pushing you to embark on an entertainment industry career quest, I strongly urge you to look at other career options.

But if you have it, then I encourage you to dedicate yourself to your quest, develop the necessary skills and information, and go for it. But be prepared and be armed. Equip yourself with as many tools, as many advantages, as much information as you can dig up in order to increase your chances of success. Ultimately, that's the core message of this book. It's a very competitive industry and you'll need every scrap of drive, determination, and knowledge—plus a bit of luck—to make it to the top. But you *can* do it.

Make the most of the opportunity when you find a responsive company, interviewer, or mentoring figure, be it a teacher, guest lecturer, or conference panelist.

Even with proper research and preparation, your career path may not go exactly as you plan. Ask the people who you know and trust if your expectations and your marketable skill set assessments are realistic. It's far better to learn now rather than later if you are basing your plans and expectations on faulty information.

I'm not suggesting you shouldn't "shoot for the stars," because if you don't aim high, you limit your own growth. But be realistic. If you dream of becoming a hit songwriter and crafting a series of Top-10 hits, go for it, but develop a "Plan B" as well. Make sure your alternate plan realistically allows you to make a living and survive as you pursue your dream. The longer the odds of accomplishing your dream, the more important it is to have a Plan B in place. Don't forget the statistic quoted earlier in the book: only one-half of one percent of the recordings released by major labels each year break even. The rest lose money for their record label.

Even after you have identified your target career path and started investigating companies, it is crucial that you continue to see yourself as an "information sponge"—someone who is hungry for every piece of information on their chosen career path. This is why reading the trade magazines, even if you can't afford to subscribe to them, is so critically important. Keeping up with the periodicals that are the "bibles" of your targeted industry will give you a big edge in your job search. Don't get lazy and give up that edge.

If you go for an informational interview at a recording studio, and you see a stack of old trade magazines, take the opportunity to politely inquire what the studio does with the back issues. It's likely that they recycle them after a few months. Offer to pick their discards up once a month and tell the receptionist that you are trying to learn all you can: "Here's my phone number. Call me and I'll come pick them up." Congratulations! You just got a pile of the magazines you need to be reading for free.

Be resourceful with respect to information gathering, especially if you're operating on limited resources. Each magazine sells for $5–$6 on a newsstand. A subscription to *Billboard* is approximately $300 a year. Remember to check for online editions, use the public or school library, and budget a set amount of time each week to be an information sponge. If you do, you will be pleasantly surprised at how much useful information, jargon, and details you retain about MRI companies and careers. Photocopy and keep the most important or insightful articles for your career book. All of this will help you position yourself as a well-informed job candidate and, upon hiring, a much more valuable member of the team.

Making Your Move

When you are armed with your resume, including as many worth points as possible, and you've done your homework by developing your marketable skill set workshops for the jobs that most interest you, and you find that your gut, geography, and salary checks all come back positive…

…then you're ready to make your move.

In the next chapter, I'll reveal the three tactics that have proven to be the most successful in seeking and obtaining a position in the entertainment industry. ⊙

The Three Best Means to Land a MRI Job

History has proven that effective networking, identifying and approaching targets of opportunity, and applying for specific help wanted listings are the key methods used to land employment in the music and recording industry. We'll review each one in this chapter.

1. Networking

Although networking was covered extensively in chapter 15, here are a few more networking tips to use in combination with that chapter's content.

Networking tips:

- Be courteous and gracious to everyone, even if they can't help you today. You never know when you may be able to support them, or they you, in the future. Remember, it is a small industry we work in.
- Carry your business cards with you all the time, even at the health spa or at a church picnic.
- If you see someone in your network and they don't recognize you, take the initiative to go up and reintroduce yourself. Never ask, "Do you remember me?" Instead say hello and let them know when you met and what you have been up to lately.
- Return calls and e-mail within twenty-four hours or the next business day.
- Nurture your network. I try to contact one person each week whom I haven't seen or chatted with recently. I also try to have lunch monthly with a person I have not seen in six months.

2. Targets of Opportunity

As part of your ongoing detective efforts, your mission is to identify any target of opportunity, a company that is established, or one that is hot and on the way up. A proactive MRI career sleuth always must be hunting for new companies that are targets of opportunity.

How do you find them? Hearing about such companies through your network is the best method. You can also scan the magazines covering the industry segments that interest you most. For the record business, *Billboard* is the right magazine to watch. Just look at page one to see which companies are regularly making the news. Also scan the Artists and Music section. If you want to be in the recording studio side of the game, then it's *Mix* magazine as well as *Billboard's* Pro Audio column and *Pro Sound News* magazine. That's how you learn about companies that are on the rise.

After identifying target companies, what's the next step? Let's say you've identified ABC Records as a hot company. Your next step is to dig up all the information you can about that company. Surf the Internet, review magazines and articles, gather clippings, and carefully read any interviews with executives of that label. Go to the library and ask the reference librarian to help you uncover articles about ABC Records.

Visit the company's Web site regularly so you know what they are doing. Go out and get every scrap of information on that label that you can. Collect it, read it, understand it. Know it backwards and forwards.

Then you're ready to send them a cold letter, one that's well written and demonstrates your worth points, along with your knowledge of their activities and your enthusiasm for the business.

Next follow up with a phone call to investigate whether or not you might be able to secure an informational interview. Better yet, find out if they are trying to fill any positions for which you may be qualified.

The worst thing you can do with a potential target of opportunity is to get in contact without being prepared to present yourself in the best light.

Better to be prepared so you can…

get **ready**
(identify companies that interest you)

and then take **aim**
(do the necessary research to understand the company and what it is doing)

then **fire!**
(open a channel of clear communication to present yourself to the company)

Anything less than that is doing yourself a disservice and is not likely to get you in the door.

Why is that? If you represent yourself poorly a few times, you're quickly diminishing your chances to make a favorable impression and to build your network with the people in the industry that could actually do you the most good. If you're in a secondary market such as San Francisco, Atlanta, Boston, Phoenix, Denver, or Austin, this is even more critical.

Be especially aware of any information that indicates growth or new areas of development for a prospective target of opportunity. Suppose one of your targets is a record label that has been very successful in r&b and now they're branching out into movie soundtracks.

Let's say you are a songwriter and have just placed one of your own songs in a locally produced film.

You could write a letter to their A&R department, introducing yourself and stating your qualifications, desire, and go-getter attitude. Mention the story in *Billboard* that alerted you to their new soundtrack division. This company may be a good target of opportunity.

Remember, for this kind of approach to bear fruit, you have to include a value statement or worth point that clearly answers the question, "what can he or she do for me today to improve my position as employer?"

Good firms are continuously on the hunt for new talent. Any company that's growing is always looking for new people. They may not be hiring that day, but savvy managers are always keeping a resume/tickler file of people with good skills. So don't ever be put off when someone says, "We're not hiring now."

Be prepared to answer that statement with, "I've studied your company, I am very interested in what you do, and I would like to ask you to please keep a copy of my resume on file in the event you need someone in the near future."

More often than not, they will accept it and may even annotate it to say, "This person has moxie or chutzpah." Bingo. At the very least, you've got yourself on file at that target of opportunity.

The most effective way to approach a target of opportunity is through a member of your network who is familiar with the company. If you don't have a personal connection, then start doing your research homework on that firm so that a direct approach via cold letter and resume may result in an informational interview for you.

3. Help Wanted Listings

Help wanted listings in the daily newspapers and music industry trade magazines are occasionally used to fill immediate job openings. Scan the trades and papers, not only for your geographic area but also nationally to see what types of jobs and skills are advertised. A help wanted listing can help you to identify which skills are required for a certain position.

The frequency of listings encountered is directly related to the type of job advertised. If you're planning to become a record producer, you are not likely to see any help wanted listings. For a songwriter, it's liable to be the same story. However, you will find help wanted listings for administrative assistants, label sales reps, royalty clerks, distribution support staff, and other positions at the mid- and entry-level.

Recording studios usually rely on word of mouth and recording schools to fill entry-level positions. For senior staffing, a referral, recommendation, or letter of introduction is more commonly employed by those seeking employment. Employers may promote from within their own company, or use their network to identify prospective candidates already working in the business.

It pays to regularly look at the help wanted listings. Remember, help wanted listings usually generate a large number of responses. If you will be responding to a listing, be sure to include a brief mention in your cover letter that you are responding to a job listing in a particular magazine or paper.

Tune up your cover letter and send your response as soon as you see the listing. This shows you are able to respond in a timely manner. It shows that you're aggressive. Always have someone proofread your cover letter. If a fax or e-mail address is listed for submitting your resume and cover letter, use it, and mail a hard copy as a backup if you have a mailing address.

Keep your cover letter as short as you can make it, and as long as it needs to be. If this is a job that you believe offers you a perfect fit, a full page is not out of the question. Why? What should you include in the cover letter? (If you don't know, reread chapter 13 now.) You must include your worth points, your experience, and what makes you a uniquely qualified candidate. Paint a word picture that positions you as the best-qualified candidate for that job. If you do, you'll reap the rewards!

If your cold or cover letter gets too wordy and overly long, there is more potential for you to hit a potential "hot button," which may be a turn-off to the person reviewing it. Remember the one-page-or-less rule when it comes to the length of such letters. Always ask yourself if you can make your points in a shorter letter. The same care that you used to prune down your resume to a tight, hard-hitting document should be spent on your cover letters.

By now, you know what your worth points are. Incorporate those that clearly communicate why you will be valuable to your next boss. Demonstrate your experience. Showcase your progressive career growth in light of your increasing levels of responsibility.

You might use a few tricks of formatting, such as bullet points or underlining a key point. Use short paragraphs, four or five of them, each covering a key point you wish to emphasize. State *specifically* which of your qualifications meet the job requirements detailed in the company's help wanted listing. This makes it easy for the screener to see that you have the required marketable skill set they are seeking. Your job is to ensure that the person reviewing your submission thinks, "Oh, he or she has experience in this area, created value here—put this one in the pile of people that we are going to call back." Following these simple guidelines will help your submission make it into the select pile that avoids the dreaded hungry shredder!

In addition to the careful wordsmithing needed, make a good visual presentation, with no typos. Make sure you don't smear the ink when it comes off the printer. If you can computer-print or type the envelope, do so. If you hand-write the envelope, do so neatly. Take your time. If you smudge it or miswrite a word, get another envelope, and make it perfect, because first impressions count for a lot.

About a week after your submission, make a follow-up phone call. Keep it short. Ask for personnel if the company has a personnel office. If it's a small firm, explain that you are calling to follow up on your resume submission for an advertised position. Ask to confirm receipt and what your next step might be. Be polite and upbeat, and respect the time of the person with whom you are speaking. The fact that you cared enough to follow up is usually viewed as a plus.

Often larger firms will send a postcard confirming receipt of your resume, stating that if they want to interview you, someone will call.

When you are starting your career, look to help wanted listings, both as opportunities that you may be able to apply for immediately, and as road signs directing you to new companies and marketable skill sets that those companies are willing to pay for.

Working all of the "big three" simultaneously—networking, targets of opportunity, and help wanted listings—is key to keeping your job search and career development on the fast track.

Follow-Up Basics: Maintaining Your Career Book, Card File, and Follow-Up System

Picture a long-distance runner as he runs a marathon. He focuses on all the little things such as maintaining an even tempo, proper breathing, knowing the course, how much water to take and when to take it, keeping his toes pointed forward, and so forth. Just as that runner has to remember each of these important details, you, as an MRI job seeker, need to develop and maintain your follow-up system.

As you develop and expand your network, increase your universe of targets of opportunity, and begin to secure interviews, you need to also:

- Attain the monthly goal you have set for expanding your network.
- Write down your new contacts and add them to your system (card file, Filofax, computer, etc.).
- Set a schedule for keeping in contact with various members of your network. Set up a section in your career book, card file, or computer database to record each contact with members of your network.
- Review your career book at least once a month and add to it regularly as you locate and mine new sources of information.
- Investigate and make contact with companies, explore new careers, and get to know the people you discover through research, reading, networking, etc.

If you have a computer, you might invest in a contact manager program such as Symantec's ACT™, or use a computer database such as Microsoft Access™, or even a spreadsheet program, to keep track of your names and contact information. An example appears below. Include the name, company name, titles and addresses, phone numbers and e-mail, date of last contact, and so forth.

Don't forget to send important people you encounter a thank-you note whenever appropriate. Performing the five follow-up basics listed above will help you maintain steady progress toward your career goal. So take them to heart, and like the long distance runner, maintain a steady pace.

CMPNY XYZ Records
FNAME Janet LNAME Doe
TITLE VP, Human Resources
ADDR1 1234 Main Street, Suite 2
CITY San Francisco STATE CA
ZIP 94124 CNTRY US
IDSTATUS1 Record Label
IDSTATUS2
IDSTATUS3
IDSTATUS4
SEND PHOTO WITH PRESS RELEASE?
PHONE (555) 555-1234 EXT
PHONE2
FAX (555) 555-5678
CEL PH
E-MAIL jdoe@xyzrecords.com
WEBSITE
ASSISTANT
REFERRED BY
COMMENTS "Met at Recording Academy Mixer in SF"
Print this Conta

As a closing note on follow-up procedures, I recently had a conversation with a human resources manager and she confirmed that *more than 50 percent of job applicants who apply for a position never bother to follow up*. That's incredible.

Don't be in that silent majority. Always take the time to follow up each application you submit to see if the position has been filled. If so, determine whether the company will keep your resume on file, and if so, for what length of time. Note that in your follow-up records. If the company is high on your list of targets, keep in touch. The results of your extra efforts may pleasantly surprise you.

Your Competition

Let's review how much competition you are likely to encounter for each of the three job search tactics we have covered in this chapter.

In the case of **networking**, your competition for specific jobs is very low because jobs identified by this method are usually not yet public knowledge. It's a fact that people often learn of jobs through their network well before they are advertised.

When you're contacting **targets of opportunity**, the competition will be a little greater, especially if it's a company with fifty or more employees. Such firms are likely to be contacted on a regular basis by savvy detectives (job seekers) like yourself.

When you approach a company in response to a **help wanted listing**, your competition will be the greatest out of the three methods, but you also know that it is 100 percent certain that the company is hiring. One person will be getting a job at the conclusion of that company's search. By following the techniques covered in this book, you will have greatly enhanced the chance that it could be you. ⦿

Job Search Technique	Level of Competition	Are They Hiring?
Networking	Low	Unknown
Targets of Opportunity	Moderate	Unknown
Help Wanted	High	Definitely

New Media Opportunities

How Information and Entertainment Are Becoming the New "Gold Standard"

A few years ago, I was surprised to learn that a young Wall Street investment counselor, David Pullman, had begun an investment fund that allowed the public to purchase shares of future earnings (appropriately called "futures") on the songs written by David Bowie.

I was fascinated by what I originally viewed as an oddity, but as time marched on, his New York–based company, The Pullman Group, signed on more and more artists willing to allow investment in their future royalty stream. Artists such as James Brown, The Isley Brothers, Ashford and Simpson, and Holland-Dozier-Holland have joined forces with Mr. Pullman. That provides a good backdrop to what I believe is rapidly becoming the new currency standard for the twenty-first century, the control and manipulation of information and entertainment. It's truly an exciting time to be involved in the music and recording business.

The Global Perspective

Roughly 38 percent of the world's population resides in two Asian countries, China and India. In 1998, the United Nations reported that Asia's overall population of 3.36 billion people represented 57 percent of the world population. In comparison, North America represents roughly 5 percent of the world population.

Most people in Asia do not speak English. However, they do listen to western music. They do play western video games. They do enjoy western movies. Entertainment today is a rapidly expanding global industry that transcends language barriers. In a recent *Billboard* article, statistics cited that U.S. copyright-related industries such as music, movies, publishing, broadcasting, and gaming made up $160 billion in revenue in the year of 1977 and grew dramatically to $530 billion in 1997. The 1997 number represents 6.3 percent of America's Gross Domestic Product (GDP) while the 1977 figure was a mere 3.6 percent of that year's GDP.

Another measure of the importance of copyright-related industries is that in the much shorter time frame of six years (1991-1997), the foreign sales of U.S.-originated, copyright-related products practically doubled from $36 billion in 1991 to $66 billion in 1997.

Statistics like these support a view I share with many future-oriented business leaders: Information has become the new gold standard.

New Media and Gaming

The same skills that apply to a career path in the music and recording industry will apply to electronic media and information-age careers. Loosely described as convergence, new media and gaming marks the intersection of information, entertainment, and business. It is where the latest technologies for the Internet, computers, cable or satellite television, broadband delivery, and music converge. Job opportunities are exploding just as fast as new companies are born and bought, as the industry races to develop and deliver the most compelling content to a worldwide audience hungry for information and entertainment.

Let's check in on one such job in the computer gaming field, that of a music composer. Forget the old notion of a sequence of a few bad-sounding synth notes repeating in an endless loop as you demolish the bad guys. Today's game, especially those delivered via CD ROM or DVD, offer well-crafted musical scores that can rival that of a feature film in sophistication, orchestration, and playback fidelity.

Music scoring for the leading game companies can be very rewarding financially. With total revenue reported at over $13 billion (source: IDSA and AMOA), the interactive game industry exceeds the $12.2 billion-a-year U.S. record business (source: RIAA, 1997 figures) and more than doubles the $5.7 billion represented by 1997 box office sales in the feature film industry.

Video games alone represent $6.2 billion in 1999 annual sales but are projected to grow to $9.3 billion in annual revenues by the year 2005 (source: Paul Kagan & Associates). Between 1997 and 1998, U.S. game revenue grew at a rate of 25 percent while U.S. box office revenue grew at 10 percent and the record business remained relatively flat. A blockbuster game such as *Mortal Kombat* racked up worldwide sales in excess of $1 billion. For a frame of reference, the movie blockbuster *Jurassic Park* took in slightly less, with $931 million worldwide revenue.

Is composing for the game industry right for everyone? Hardly. But if you are a talented composer who is comfortable working with computer and MIDI programs, you should investigate your opportunities. Long hours and critical deadlines can lead to some all-nighters for those in this field, but the rewards outstrip those available to the band playing covers in the lounge at the local Holiday Inn.

Staff positions as a music composer at the larger software developers pay in the $45,000–$70,000 range with benefits, paid holidays, and profit-sharing programs. Freelancers working for game developers can also do well on a project-by-project basis.

And not just composers are needed. Any skill or craft that goes into the making of a feature film is likely to be required when a new game is on the drawing board: session musicians, recording engineers, dialog editors, voice talent, computer graphics designers, sound effects editors, production assistants, continuity, video editors, localization experts, and on and on.

I encourage you to also look beyond gaming to Internet audio, video, and broadcasting, electronic learning aids, and other media that utilize audio, music recording, and sound editing. Check out software development, content generation, and programming for the emerging 500+ channels of content that are on the horizon for home delivery (cable, broadband, and satellite). You'll see that literally dozens of new opportunities are being developed each week. Dive in and start exploring.

Another very hot area is the issue of rights protection, watermarking, and digital delivery of media to the consumer. Look for careers in this area to continue to grow at an amazing pace as newer, faster, and more secure technologies emerge. Another area will be international relations and distribution deals in a global marketplace where borders and laws are difficult to enforce due to the explosion of the Internet.

Companies are working harder than ever before to maximize the earning potential of each new entertainment vehicle. Movie tie-ins, tour sponsorships, sheet music folios, soundtrack albums such as *Titanic*, *Prince of Egypt*, and *Austin Powers*, to name a few recent hits, and made-for-TV movies on the lives of rockers, all present new and potentially lucrative earning opportunities for a wide range of MRI personnel.

Force yourself to think out of the box. There's a great big beautiful world in the entertainment industry for those who are motivated to make their mark. Push yourself to look beyond the record company or recording studio and at least explore the potential for what creative and financial opportunities may exist in these exciting new media market segments.

TAKING CHARGE OF YOUR OWN CAREER DEVELOPMENT

If you've taken the steps outlined in this book, you're armed to start your trek to the top. Rather than give you a pep talk, here are a few reminders to help keep you focused as you begin your career journey.

- Make sure that your resume is rock solid. Take pride in knowing that a top-notch resume sets you apart from the vast majority of job seekers. Take the time to fine tune a cover letter that clearly states why you are writing and how hiring *you* can improve your future employer's business!
- Employ all three tactics simultaneously to uncover jobs and companies that interest you: networking, contacting targets of opportunity, reading, and responding to any help wanted position listings that are appropriate.
- Prepare yourself mentally and spiritually for the rejection that comes with any job search. Unfortunately, rejection is a basic part of the weeding-out process that is so central to the entertainment industry. Many doors will be closed to you, but it only takes one to open to establish a career beachhead.
- Maintain a positive attitude. When the going gets really tough, rely on members of your network to help you maintain focus on where you are headed and to remind you of how far you have already progressed.
- Set short-, medium- and long-range goals and measure your progress towards attaining them. Regardless of whether you have landed your dream job, doing so will give you a sense of accomplishment.
- Learn to ask intelligent questions. When it comes time for an interview or furthering a relationship with a member of your network, you need to be perceived as an asset, not a liability. Learning to research and develop intelligent questions about a career path or an area of interest is a proven means to set you apart from other job seekers.
- As you network with people and secure informational interviews, you will become more and more connected to your local entertainment community. Members of your network will land jobs, get promotions, and move up. You must keep in touch with them.

- Invest the necessary time required to do research. Become a thorough detective and do your career homework so you become well versed in your area of interest.
- Identify those companies who are the leaders in the sector of the market you're interested in. Find out as much as you can about each one.
- Locate a willing mentor or sponsor to help you along your career path. They can be an instructor, teacher, retired professional, journalist, a family member or relative, a neighbor, or acquaintance who takes an interest in your quest and can provide insight and share life experiences. There is no substitute for a working knowledge of the industry in which you plan to work. Fast track your career development by getting as much industry and networking experience as you can.

The last fact to keep in mind is that tens of thousands of other people have gone before you on the road to a fulfilling career in the music, recording, and entertainment business. They've gotten their careers started from a small opportunity. They've made the investment in time, energy, and self-improvement to build a career in one of the most exciting industries in the world.

You can do it, too. ⊙

part five

Views from the Top

To offer additional insights into careers in the music and recording industry, four professionals have shared their views on career development and requirements for success in today's music recording world.

- *Leslie Ann Jones, Director of Music Recording and Scoring at Skywalker Sound*
- *Murray Allen, Vice President of Post Production, Electronic Arts, Inc.*
- *Gary and Joan Gand, Music Retailers and Owners of Gand Music & Sound*
- *Gregg Hildebrandt, Northern California Sales Rep for the TASCAM, a Division of TEAC of America*

An Interview with Leslie Ann Jones Director of Music Recording and Scoring at Skywalker Sound

Leslie Ann Jones is Director of Music Recording and Scoring at Skywalker Sound, the recording and production facilities built by George Lucas in Marin County, California. She has been a recording and mixing engineer for twenty-five years, during which time she has worked with such artists as Herbie Hancock, Angela Bofill, Michael Feinstein, Michelle Shocked, BeBe & CeCe Winans, Bobby McFerrin, Holly Near, Rosemary Clooney, and Narada Michael Walden. She launched her film score mixing career with Francis Ford Coppola's *Apocalypse Now*.

Starting her career at L.A.'s ABC Studios in 1975, she joined the staff of San Francisco's famed Automatt Recording Studios from 1978–1987. Next up was a ten-year post at Hollywood's Capitol Studios. Leslie returned to Northern California in 1997 to accept her current position at Skywalker Sound.

In addition to her work recording and mixing music albums and film scores at Skywalker, Leslie also serves as the Chairwoman of the Recording Academy, the 14,000-member trade organization responsible for the Grammy awards and numerous other educational initiatives.

Keith: What drew you to music or recording initially?

Leslie: Well, I guess it's because I grew up in the music business, because my parents were performers and I was a guitar player. I just kind of progressed from that. I actually was drawn to music first, then the recording business later.

K: What can you share about your first paying gig in the business?

L: Well, as a recording engineer, I was working for ABC Records, which was owned by the ABC Television Network. They had a recording studio.

I'd already done a lot of live sound and had taken a couple of recording engineer courses, which were the first offered in L.A. I actually wanted to be a record producer and manager; I wanted to emulate Peter Asher. I didn't really plan on being an engineer. But I thought I should learn something about engineering, to make me a better producer/manager.

So I just went and asked. I knew the studio manager, Phil Kaye. I told him I wanted the job, and he said, "Well, there aren't any other women doing what you want to do. I don't know how it will work, so we'll just see how the clients react to you. We'll just have to play it by ear."

K: What background, training, or education has proven helpful for you during your career?

L: Let's see, I think reading a lot proved really helpful. Most people that go into this line of work have at least some sort of natural inclination for either the music or the technology.

As I said, the two recording classes that I took were the first offered in L.A., and mostly for me it was because I was so self-taught that I really needed to double-check what I thought I knew.

But I started out reading magazines like *Stereo Review* and *Hi-Fidelity* because there was no *Mix* magazine when I started out.

Many people came to it from kind of a broadcast or Heath Kit home electronic background. Many of your readers may not even know what Heath Kit is. Heath Kit was a catalog company in the 1950s–1970s that provided home electronics kits for ham radio and hi-fi enthusiasts to build their own equipment.

K: Heath Kit is important to many engineers of our vintage because it provided the hands-on aspect.

L: Absolutely.

K: I think many of us got those little kits, those "Build an AM Radio Kit" on our ninth birthday or whatever. I can do this, you know. They provided a breadboard, soldering iron, parts list, instructions, and off we went.

L: Well, yes. Those classes helped me a lot because by the time I got the job at ABC, which was essentially making tape copies on an eight-hour shift, I had already learned quite a bit about sound.

I was familiar enough with tape machines so that no one had to point and say, "That's a seven-inch reel, that's a ten-inch reel." I wasn't terribly nervous and I understood the basic process of recording.

I sometimes think now what happens is kids learn too much, and when they go into their first job, they're not able to keep an open mind.

I feel that some of the schools forget or don't spend enough time on the fundamentals. Instead they emphasize learning how to run Pro Tools or an SSL (Solid State Logic) board.

And then, of course, they get to their first job and the place doesn't use either one. So don't overlook the importance of really mastering the basics.

K: Were there any early mentors who influenced you?

L: There were many. I kept a really open mind and I asked a lot of questions. I was very eager to learn and jump right in and do new things. I was the person who raised my hand whenever there was an opportunity to take on something new. When you do that, people naturally start to feed you more information.

But I would say my first main mentor was [engineer and producer] Roy Halee. And then after that, it would be [engineer] Fred Catero and [producer] David Rubinson.

L: When I met Roy, he was head of A&R for ABC Records. And he came from CBS/Columbia Records. And actually he and Fred had both worked together in New York in the '50s and '60s. And then Roy moved to California and Fred moved to San Francisco.

Roy had engineered and produced Simon & Garfunkel, among many other great artists such as Blood Sweat & Tears, Bob Dylan, Journey, Laura Nyro, Boz Scaggs, and Paul Simon. When I worked with Roy, he was working with Rufus and other artists signed to ABC.

And Fred, of course, recorded Janis Joplin, Santana, Herbie Hancock,

The Pointer Sisters—every kind of major artist that was representative of the San Francisco sound—as well as Barbra Streisand, Bob Dylan, Chicago, and other CBS artists.

David Rubinson was the producer who developed many of those acts, and he and Fred were a team working together out of the Automatt [now a parking lot at Fourth and Folsom in San Francisco].

K: Now fast-forward to the present day. We mentioned your official job title. Let's talk a little bit about your role in the day-to-day workings of Skywalker, because I understand you wear a couple of different hats in your job.

L: Well, I not only run the studio but I'm responsible for every aspect of the recording operations: booking the studio, the administration, the budget, the personnel, hiring/firing, buying equipment—all of that.

I help to steer it and market the scoring facility. Really, the scoring stage operates like any small business.

Plus, I'm still a recording engineer. So although I don't record every session, I do record about 30 percent of what goes on here.

K: What part of your job gives you the most satisfaction?

L: Obviously, the studio work is always very satisfying. But it's easy to get burned out when you do too much of it, which is why I chose to pursue a job that is a bit different, but one that is still rewarding and a lot of fun. Whether I'm the engineer or not, I really enjoy when people have a great time here.

L: However, I would say that being in the room when a great performance is happening is still the main thing that inspires me.

K: Could you describe an entry-level position at Skywalker?

L: On the scoring stage, that gig is as a runner, which we have now although it's not a full-time position. The runner is just called in on an as-needed basis, because we only have the one music studio.

L: For the rest of the Skywalker facilities [home to the post production and mixing stages for hundreds of hit movies, as well as special effects division, Industrial Light and Magic], most people come in as central machine room operators (MRO) for the mix stage. Sometimes they might come in as transfer people, as well. But that requires quite a bit more experience and education.

A transfer op may have been somebody who worked at a smaller facility for a year or two, got their feet wet, and knows the difference between a single stripe and dual stripe mag, drop-frame and non-drop-frame time code, and so forth.

K: Could you identify three attributes or skills—it could be either—that you would look for in an entry-level person?

L: I think we tend to gravitate towards people that have the right amount of enthusiasm.

We don't have a lot of people working here, and there isn't any formal time period that you're going to stay in each job. It just seems that those people that tend to excel at what they do, who grow and progress through the organization—start as a mix tech and progress to a mixer—are the ones that have the most self-motivation. They can think for themselves, they are smart, and they invest the time to educate themselves.

I really think not knowing too much and not knowing too little is key. I mean, even for a runner, the guy we have now studied for a number of years at Berklee College of Music in Boston.

I don't have to worry about him knowing the etiquette in the room or being unfamiliar with equipment. He has a really strong music background. Yet he doesn't know so much that he expects to walk in and be an assistant engineer right away. He's willing to make food runs and do whatever it takes to keep the session running, just so he can be here.

But there are only so many jobs, so you have to be flexible and be willing to fit in wherever you can. You need to stay attuned to the opportunities that might present themselves and be willing to jump in and take a chance. That's what I've done in the last twenty-five years—let's see, I've had five jobs. This is my fifth job.

And one of those jobs is counting the three years I spent as an independent engineer. I am pleased to say that, in each of my jobs, I have gone past what I thought I knew or tried something kind of different, with an element of risk. Realizing that the next career move wasn't necessarily safe. That's the only way you can really grow.

And that risk/growth relationship is a preview of what you're going to have to do when you finally sit in the chair as an engineer anyway. You are going to have to get past whatever knowledge you have to when the client says, "That's too orange." You have to figure out what that means and how to make the track sound more "green."

You should know enough about what you're doing and the tools that you have available to you to creatively get the job done.

K: What is the salary range for an entry-level position?

L: Well, interns get paid less than staff positions, although they do get paid. It is anywhere from $10–$18 per hour depending on what the person will be doing.

K: When a person is getting started in the business, they are there to primarily learn—not so much to earn. Try to get into a good learning situation, because the money comes later.

L: Yeah. Actually, that's why I really recommend that a person get a job in the biggest studio they can find and not take a job in a one-room place. Chances are, they're not going to really learn in a one-room studio.

K: Skywalker has an internship program. Could you talk about it briefly?

L: Well, it is handled through our human resources department. First a department like ours must decide each year whether or not to request an intern because the salary to pay the intern comes out of each department's budget.

And then if anyone applied for an internship with the scoring stage as his or her preference, then we would probably get one.

L: But every company is different. Some do it like Capitol Records, where they would hire six interns from local music business programs throughout L.A., and they would spend a week in each department.

K: You mentioned you have a runner/intern now on the scoring stage. Can you estimate what percentage of new hires are current or former interns?

L: Around 20 percent.

K: Do you have any tips you can offer to somebody who is thinking about getting into the business? When you started, you walked in and approached Phil Kaye at ABC and said, "I'd like to engineer here." Things are quite a bit different now, obviously.

L: Yes, I think they are different. A lot of people that we consider tend to come recommended from other people in the business. We also have a relationship with certain schools. I might e-mail the head of the recording department asking if they have any outstanding students, which is exactly what I did the last time we were looking for somebody.

I contacted Los Medanos, San Francisco State, and Berklee College of Music and just asked if anyone had a couple of bright young kids. A referral like that is one way to get a start.

The other way is just to call around, and if somebody says they're not hiring, send them a resume and follow it up with another call. Or, you can ask if you can come by, drop off your resume, and see the studio. That way, the person who is hiring gets a chance to meet you, even though they might not be thinking about it at the time.

That approach may not work at some facilities that just do not have time or availability to accommodate drop-in visitors, but for many studios, it *will* work, so it's worth a try.

You should ask, "May I stop by and drop off my resume and meet you, and spend about five minutes speaking with you?" Studio managers are generally very busy people, but at least you've had the opportunity to meet a person in the music community and hopefully make a favorable impression.

K: As far as resources, is there anything you think someone coming into the business should be looking at?

L: Well, I think for somebody just starting out, *Mix* might be a little too much. I guess *Recording* or *EQ* magazine might be a better place to start.

We haven't yet talked about knowing computers, either. You certainly don't have to know Pro Tools editing, but you really should know the fundamentals of either a Mac or a PC. I think having some knowledge of hard disk editing is quite an advantage.

I would also suggest joining the Recording Academy as an associate or as an affiliate member, because you still have access to any of the workshops that are offered once you're on the mailing list. A lot of those events are free. So the networking and educational opportunities available in that organization are available whether you're a voting member or not.

A lot of schools have student AES (Audio Engineering Society) chapters; I know San Francisco State does.

As far as conventions, I would think now, NAMM would be a good place to go to learn a little bit about who the players are in the technology side of recording.

K: Long term, what's your sense of the career opportunity represented by becoming a recording engineer?

L: Well, I think it can still be a [good] career opportunity, but I know that even well-respected veteran engineers are learning Pro Tools or some other hard disk editing system, because clients are kind of expecting that and they want that available to them. Colleagues of mine have said, "Why should they pay someone else [to do hard disk editing,] when they can pay me?"

So that's certainly job security. I'm still pretty bullish on that, but I think there are many opportunities out there with distribution changing with the Internet, uploading, and new technologies.

K: Do you have any parting thoughts?

L: Master the basics and the fundamentals.

I think that's the big advantage of working in a big place and not in a small place—you're exposed to a lot more. In my nine years at Capitol, I was pushed to do so many things, not only the level of clientele that we had, but just kind of the things we were asked to do. All the Frank Sinatra *ednet* ISDN sessions for the two *Duets* albums happened at Capitol. Then we shifted gears to record a film score with a large orchestra at the next session. You wouldn't really get that kind of experience in a one-room studio. It makes you much more valuable as an employee because eventually, you are going to have to look for another job. It always happens.

K: It's true. A person's depth of knowledge makes them much more valuable to their employer.

Do you have any Yoda-like pearls of wisdom to share in closing?

L: Use your ears, Luke—use your ears. ⦿

An Interview with Murray Allen
Vice President of Post Production
Electronic Arts, Inc.

Murray Allen's career spans more than fifty years in the music and entertainment industry. He has been a musician, producer, session player, studio owner, and studio designer, and now serves as Vice President of Post Production for one of the world's most successful electronic gaming companies, Electronic Arts, based in Redwood City, CA.

During the golden era of big bands, he played sax and clarinet with the Glenn Miller, Sauter Finegan, Bobby Sherwood, and Skitch Henderson bands. Murray backed up artists including Frank Sinatra, Tony Bennett, Frankie Laine, and Perry Como. His session work includes dates with Stevie Wonder, The Platters, and Andy Williams.

When the guitar began to rule pop music, Murray started to engineer recording sessions, rapidly becoming one of the most in-demand engineers in Chicago, recording the likes of Ramsey Lewis, Duke Ellington, Steve Allen, Stan Kenton, and Sammy Davis, Jr. In the early '70s, he became president of Universal Recording, where he would stay for the next seventeen years. During that time, the studio won numerous Emmy and Grammy nominations, and compiled a substantial number of Clio awards (the Oscar-equivalent of the advertising industry).

Murray's insatiable quest for knowledge and love of technology led Universal to many "firsts" in the recording industry: pioneering the use of digital audio workstations in commercial production; offering video sweetening (in 1971) before SMPTE time code was developed; and mentoring other studio owners and managers in recording studio management.

During Murray's watch at Universal, more than 250 feature film and television soundtracks were recorded by the studio staff including: *Steel Magnolias*, *Home Alone*, *Flatliners*, *The Witches of Eastwick*, *Brighton Beach Memoirs*, *Sea of Love*, *Midnight Run*, and many more. In its heyday, Universal employed more than 400 employees.

In his current position, he heads up audio and video post production, quality assurance, testing, and customer service for Electronic Arts. He has been sound designer of the Grammy awards telecast for twenty years, and an active member of the Recording Academy and SPARS.

Murray is a man with a boundless supply of energy, an uncanny ability to identify and develop new talent, and a passion for excellence in everything he undertakes. One quote from Murray sums up his apparent ability to do just about anything to which he sets his mind: *"I'm not concerned with problems, I'm only concerned with solutions."*

Keith: What drew you to the music and recording business?

Murray: Well, it's a funny story. I started playing an instrument when I was about six years old. I started on piano, and then I migrated over to clarinet when I was eight years old. But my first love was physics. I really loved being an engineer and doing all kinds of stuff that related to physics.

When I was in high school, however, everybody had to take swimming, and I've always been afraid of the water. So the only way you could get out of swimming was to be in the military band. Now because I already played clarinet pretty well, I joined the military band. So I became a musician because I had a fear of water.

Later on when I got out of high school, I went to Illinois Institute of Technology (IIT) because I wanted to be a physicist. That was my goal. But I already was a working musician. I'd been working as a musician since I was about thirteen years old. I had my own Society Band at the Morraine Hotel on Chicago's North Shore when I was sixteen years old.

When I was enrolled at IIT in the 1940s, an engineer with a masters degree working on the Manhattan Project was earning about $7,500 a year. As a musician I was already making $8,000 a year.

So I thought, why do I want to spend all this time getting an advanced degree in physics, even though I love it, to earn less money? Coming up through the Depression, money has been a very important motivation for me.

So I then became a professional musician. I went to New York. I wanted to study from Joe Allard, who was considered the best clarinet/saxophone teacher in the country at that time. And when I was there I got to play a little bit on the Calvacade of Bands, WOR radio, and I worked full-time at Roseland Ballroom as a lead saxophone player. And then I was going to be drafted for the Korean War.

So I came back and I went to college to stay out of the draft. And I finally got tired of that. So I enlisted in the army. I figured I should get it out of the way. But because I enlisted in the army, I was able to choose my duty station and I joined the Fifth Army Band. Next, I got myself a radio show that we did five days a week. We did it with my own five-piece band. And my piano player for three years was the incomparable Bill Evans.

I was stationed near Chicago, and during that time, I started moonlighting playing record dates. It was highly illegal and definitely against the regulations. But I did it and I never got caught.

So by the time I got out of the army, I went on the road with a band to work at the Hilton chain for about a year, after which I took my own band into the Conrad Hilton Hotel in Chicago.

I was there for two years, and I was working record dates and everything else. Then finally I had so many record dates, that's all I did. I became a full-time studio musician. I did that from about 1956–57, all the way through to the mid-1960s. I recorded hundreds of albums and singles.

Anyway, around 1965 I could see that rock 'n' roll was starting to come in. Where I used to work about twenty-seven sessions per week, it was getting down to maybe twenty. I've always kept charts and graphs on whatever I was doing. Got down to about twenty sessions a week, and then about fifteen. We used to have about five saxophone players in every session, Henry Mancini-type arrangements. We were getting down to three or four saxes.

Well, I was the number-two call, so I always worked. But I thought I needed to make a decision. I've either got to learn to engineer again, or I have to learn to play the guitar. One of the two.

Backtracking a bit to my time in New York in the early 1950s, I worked the Roseland Ballroom. We had air shots every night where we broadcast over CBS and ABC, and then NBC.

The next day I'd go over to the station and listen to a playback of what we did. They used to record it. I sounded terrible.

So I went over to Manny's Music store one day and I bought an Ampex tape recorder and speakers, amplifiers, and microphones. It took me three years to pay for it, but I learned how to use it and how to make a decent recording. Having a science background, it was no big deal. I learned how to mix, record, and take the machine apart and put it back together again. I knew how to repair it and keep it running just right.

So consequently then, going back to the mid-1960s, I decided to get back into recording. I knew what makes an Ampex recorder work. I knew about mixing. So I started mixing a few dates and all of a sudden, clients wanted me to start mixing for them.

Well, because I was making so much money in residuals playing on commercials, I said, "The only way I'll work for you as a mixer is if you also hire me as a musician." So they started doing that.

What happened then is that I became *extremely* busy. The other mixer in Chicago at that time was a man named Bruce Swedien. Now Bruce was going to work for another company in Chicago, but he had a one-year no-compete clause. So for one year, I became the number-one mixer.

I was mixing sessions at RCA, CBS, and at Universal in the morning, and recording music. But in the afternoon, they were taking the 8-track tapes back over to Universal or some other place to finish. They put the announcers on and did the final mix.

I didn't get a piece of that action. I was only getting the music part. So two other engineers and myself opened up a studio called "Audio Finishers," a real hole-in-the-wall. But, then we added some experimental acoustic treatment to it, and we called it the Audio Finishers so that we could do that finishing work in the afternoon.

But then RCA in Chicago closed down for a year because they wanted to move, and Curtis Mayfield and all these Chicago acts needed a place to record. Well, it turns out that at this time we got the first 16-track recorder in Chicago.

Acoustically the place was great for stacking [overdubbing], since it had great separation. So all of a sudden we started getting all the Curtis Mayfield work, Donnie Hathaway, Roberta Flack, and we started "stealing" business from CBS and from Universal, because the sound of our little room was so good. Plus, we had the only 16-track in town. And because we were good mixers, we got great sounds.

Universal came to us and said that we were killing them. They asked if we could enter into some type of agreement. We knew that our studio was limited in what it could do, because it was so small. Universal had such large, great sounding rooms.

So we made a deal with Universal. One thing led to another and eventually we took over management in 1970, then bought the studio in 1975. I still was working sessions, by the way, and engineering. I was going back and forth between the two studios.

The rest is history. We quickly became a gigantic operation—a major studio. We were nominated three times for TEC awards. We did over 250 feature films. We did every note of music in the original *Blues Brothers* film, which I'm very proud of. We had a cassette manufacturing plant working under contract for CBS and Motown. At that time, we had more than 400 employees.

But a funny thing happened. After twelve years running Universal, around 1985, I started getting very tired of running a recording studio. I hate to admit this, but we started getting to where everything was stacked one track at a time. We didn't use big orchestras anymore. Producers who were getting into the business now were not musicians. Computer programming was the coming wave for pop music production.

And although we were the first studio to do so many things, I was getting very bored. We had to spend so much money just to keep up with the competition, it was terrible.

So I decided to get out of the studio business. I sold the company in 1989 and I stayed on for about another year. And then I was a consultant for about a year. I worked with Editel [one of the leading post production houses] in Chicago.

I also worked with Tom Kobayashi who left Lucas Arts at that time and founded *ednet*. I helped him work with Crescent Moon Studios down in Florida, and put in a T1 line between them and Capitol Studios in Los Angeles—so that Gloria Estefan could do her Christmas album from her home in Florida and the band could play live in California.

Phil Ramone was the producer. Phil and I have worked together for so many years. That technology is what kicked off the Sinatra *Duets* album, which was the first chart topper that proved that artists could collaborate over T1 or ISDN lines from anywhere in the world. The artist, producer, and musicians no longer had to be in the same studio.

K: How did you make the move to Electronic Arts?

M: One day the phone rang and it was a headhunter asking me, "Murray, would you like to go out and live in California?" He said there's a job opening at Electronic Arts, and I came out here and I interviewed. Silicon Valley in 1993 closely resembled the record business back in the early 1950s. So I said, "Yes, this is going to be fun." And that's how I got to where I am today.

K: Do you remember your first paying gig?

M: When I was thirteen, we used to go out and play at the local park districts. Whatever they collected at the door we split among the band. So we would get $2–$3 each, or something like that.

Actually, when I was about twelve years old, I was on a radio show in Chicago called "The Joe Kelly Quiz Kids Band." We did a couple of shows. We didn't get paid for it because in those days, the musician's union was extremely strong.

K: Sure. You couldn't be paid without membership in the union.

M: That's right. And we couldn't join the union until we were sixteen. So they gave us a waiver. They had to have a bunch of musicians stand by and get paid while we did the actual playing. But the first actual payment I got was these little park-concert-type things.

K: You mentioned earlier that you had loved science and had studied it avidly both in high school and afterwards at the Illinois Institute of Technology. That obviously came in handy when you bought your first Ampex tape recorder.

M: Well, I understood about electronics and signal flow, because I had a scientific type of mind. I still do to this day. In order words, I do not want anybody telling me, "This does not work." Instead, let's see why it doesn't work, and let's figure out how we make it work. I'm not concerned with problems; I am only concerned with solutions.

K: You mentioned a couple of people early on who were influences on you. Is there anyone in particular?

M: Well, Bill Putnam was a big influence, actually because he built Universal. Bill Putnam, Bernie Clapper, and Bob Weber came out of the service, and they were up in Evanston, Illinois.

They started a business doing time-delay broadcasting. They got the contract from ABC, it was then called the Blue Network, to do these time-delay broadcasts.

So the performances that were broadcast in New York would come over the phone lines to them in Evanston. They then recorded it on 16-inch transcription disks.

The performance would be rebroadcast in Chicago at the appropriate time. ABC at that time had a studio on top of the Civic Opera building. Part of their deal was that Bill and his partners could use this studio to do some music recording, which they wanted to do.

There were about fifteen guys that were the original owners of Universal Recording. One of them was a guy named Jerry Bradley. He owned a club in Chicago, a nightclub called the 5100 Club. He was the one that introduced me to Danny Thomas, who was the comedian at his club.

This was before television became so popular, and everybody would go out at night to a club and drink. Anyway, Bradley's son went to high school with me. We had a high school band, and we were to break-in the studio, Universal, to see how it sounded.

Our high school band went up there and we recorded at Universal, atop the Civic Opera House. And I remember the tune we recorded was "A Starry Night." Da da da da da da [Murray hums the melody]… by Tchaikovsky. Those were fun days, in 1946.

Anyway, Bill Putnam was the engineer. That's where I first met Bill. Now later on they did the Harmonicats up there. "Peg of My Heart," which was a huge hit record. That's where they used the "john" for the echo chambers. Bill was an influence on me, from an engineering point of view, early on.

A lot of guys influenced me early in my life when I was on the road. Like Morrie Feld, who was the drummer with the Benny Goodman Sextet for many years.

When I was on the road, I was in the backup band for Frankie Laine, and the drummer and my roommate was Morrie. He taught me about the importance of rhythm and time in jazz. Another one was Joe Daly, a Chicago saxophone player. He and I were roommates in a lot of bands. He was a great jazz player. Mel Lewis, Louis Bellson, and Peter Erskine all had a musical impact on me.

And, of course, Bill Evans [the great jazz pianist] was a tremendous influence; I enjoyed working with him every night for three years.

K: Now fast-forward to today. Tell me a bit about what you do at Electronic Arts.

M: From an audio and video [production] point of view, I try and keep people [moving] back towards the center. There's a natural tendency for younger people to try to experiment. They all have tastes, but many don't realize what makes a production really work. So try and keep things aimed towards the center, knowing that if it doesn't have that magic, it doesn't mean a damn thing.

In any sort of audio or visual production, you have to have a vision for what the project will come out like, and go with it—I hate committees.

K: Meaning, you should have a vision and stick with it.

M: Yes, and pick the right people to get the job done. You know, not everybody may agree that this is the best way of doing it, but as long as you are in what I call that "window of acceptability"—you're cool.

K: So some of your time is spent as a coach? Mentoring to some degree?

M: I do a lot of mentoring. That's probably the biggest thing I do at Electronic Arts. But I have 300 people working for me, so a lot of it is just making decisions on: How do we handle this? What do we do about this?

The most important lesson I try to impress on my staff is to never use the word "no." I do not want anybody to say, "We can't do this." I want them to say, "Well, let's think about this. Let's see what it will take to get the job done right." Whether it is about money, people, or whatever is required. Then you can make the decision; if it's too costly, you don't do it.

K: What aspect of your current role at Electronic Arts do you enjoy the most?

M: Building teams. I've built a number of teams in the time I've been here. I was given the assignment of starting a customer support team. This was three and a half years ago. We are now considered to be the best technical support group in the whole business.

Management asked me to develop a product-testing team. When I started the testing team, I had two people. I now have 150 people on the testing team and we did sixty-two titles this year. Today's games have a great deal of depth, so testing is a complex process.

K: Building these teams is obviously something you enjoy greatly.

M: Well, that's what I did at Universal. I like to build teams, build loyalty. I believe that to be a leader, you have to first have been a follower. In other words, before you can play first saxophone, you have got to spend a lot of years playing second saxophone. So you know what it takes to be part of a team and make it work. Once you do that, the most important thing is being honest, being fair, and being consistent.

I stress that you must be honest, you must be fair, you must be consistent, and you must have a passion for what you do. If you don't have a passion, you should get out of the business right now.

K: What's an entry-level position like at Electronic Arts? What would somebody be doing there when they started out?

M: In my groups, most people start off in technical support. First, they have to pass a test, and then go through a rigorous three-week training program, and we send them back to school to learn about what we do. Next, they go through a two-week, hands-on mentoring and polishing process.

At that point, they're ready to get on the phone solving problems for our customers—which is the toughest job in the world.

But through that, they learn what our customer needs. It's very important that you always listen to your customer. If you don't listen to your customer, you are in deep trouble.

In other words, they develop a dialog with the customers and they develop a skill for understanding what our customers need—how the games work. Of course all these persons are avid gamers, so that's another requirement.

K: I guess there's no shortage of gamers!

M: No. And then from there they move on to testing. And from testing they may move into production, marketing, or the online division. However, it all starts at the beginning, the customer equation. Essentially, it is all about the product and the customer.

K: How about people working in audio or video production?

M: We bring experienced people in. My mixer, I hired from Universal Studios in L.A. I recruited my video staff from a post production company. People have got to get their experience from somewhere else and come to us as a journeyman, not an apprentice. We haven't got time for training with our production schedules.

K: On the audio side they're going to know the basics of Pro Tools. They're going to know the basics of samplers or sequencers…

M: A lot more than basics. I mean they have to have experience, credits where they've been successful in the studio, and the same goes for video.

K: Can you tell me the salary range for an entry-level person?

M: When someone starts out in technical support, they get started at anywhere between $10 to $12 an hour. First as temp employees, and then, when they get hired, they may be at $25,000 to $27,000 a year.

K: That's pretty good for entry level.

M: Well down here [in Silicon Valley] it isn't. There are companies down here that start people at $17 per hour because of such a tight labor market.

But down here in the Valley, we have 1 percent unemployment at the bottom end [entry-level]. At the top end, we have zero unemployment right now.

K: Do you have any type of program where students who are in their final year of school or college can be exposed to what goes on…

M: We have a full-time staff that does this. And we actually go to the universities. We have recruiters that go out. We bring in interns. We have co-op programs. Sure. We do all of that. And the interns we recruit are paid positions.

K: Can you estimate what percentage of new hires are former or current interns?

M: I'm not sure what the percentage is, and it's usually programmers. We go to Stanford, MIT, and various other schools. We look for programmers and artists, but mainly programmers.

We give them a project during the summer, and if they do well with it, we try and get them back the next summer. When they graduate, we try and hire them.

K: Are there any tips that you could share for someone wanting to enter the recording or interactive music business, to help them get their foot in the door?

M: First of all, you've got to decide what do you want to do. In other words, if you want to make money, then you should go into the banking business or to Wall Street or Montgomery Street here in San Francisco. If you want to sell jewelry, then work on 47th Street in New York City.

However, if you want to be in music, either go to L.A., New York, or Nashville. I prefer New York or Los Angeles. *Wherever there's* ***more*** *competition, you'll have* ***more*** *opportunity.* Never go to a place where there's no competition because there's no opportunity for you there.

K: That is a very important point.

M: Also, whatever you end up doing, you've got to learn to do better, at least in your own mind. You have to do it better than anybody else in the world does.

When I interview people here, I always ask the question, "What do you do better than anybody else in the world?" Pick one thing. I don't care what it is, but what do you do better than anybody else in the world?

The person must have enough self-esteem to really feel that they indeed do something better than somebody else. Now maybe they really do, which is even better. I also ask them to make up a "balance sheet" on their strong points and their weak points. Are you honest? Honesty is absolutely critical. It is important that a person doesn't lie, doesn't cheat, or isn't devious.

And you hang out. You have to hang out with the people that you ultimately want to work with. So if you want to be a songwriter and work with rock bands, get a copy of *Billboard*. Find out all about rock bands and who their publishers are. Start calling them. Get to know their names. Learn their secretary's names. You should learn the people's names that are in the flow of that business.

When you go talk to them the first time, say, "That last record you did was the greatest thing. I love those lyrics." So that they know you are interested in them and what they do. If you're lucky, they'll do the rest of the talking and you'll be hired!

K: It's really true. Show people you have an interest in what they're doing and often times they want to open up to you.

M: That's right. Let them do the talking and they're more likely to hire you.

K: Are there any magazines, books, articles, or organizations that people who want to get into the business should keep their eye on?

M: It's all on the Web now—just start surfing. You've also got to start looking for job sites on the Web—there's so many of them.

But basically you should focus yourself. Decide what you want to do and how you want to do it. Just aim in that direction and work at it.

It may take you a month, it may take you two years, or it might take you five years. But when you get there, you've got what you want.

However, don't put a timetable on your career. You may not hit the heights right away… Richard Strauss didn't start writing good music until he was fifty years old.

My goal is to hit the peak of my career about a day before I die. *[Laughter.]*

K: Hopefully that will be many years in the future, Murray, from what I can foretell.

M: Only God and myself will know, and I'm not going to talk. *[More laughter.]*

K: What's your glimpse into the future? Will entertainment media continue evolving?

M: Oh yeah, sure. Yeah, it has to. To just be competitive, sure.

Television is going to change with 2,000 channels. There's a lot of opportunity there.

M: I hope the quality improves, with most of the music on TV it's gotten so bad. It's because people get out of college and they have Pro Tools or some kind of a sampler. They start creating music without any experience. And the producers that hire them have no experience either.

One thing I preach is that [good] music has to be entertaining music. It's got to hit you in the nerves. It's got to make you want to get up and dance. It's got to make your whole body want to shake.

And if it doesn't do that—then there's always an opportunity for somebody who truly has the intuitive talent to create good music and good audio. And boy if you have it, then we need you! ⊙

An Interview with Gary Gand
President of Gand Music & Sound
Northfield, Illinois

Gary and Joan Gand own and operate Gand Music & Sound in Northfield, IL, a suburb of Chicago. They have been a husband-and-wife team for more than thirty years, first playing in the same band and eventually opening a small guitar shop that has grown into one of the premiere music and recording retail stores in North America.

My interview with Gary (Joan was unavailable the day of our interview) clearly demonstrates the passion, commitment, and drive a person must have to get to the top of the music business. Gary's multifaceted career includes stints as a performer, session musician, guitar repair whiz, engineer, and now president of a retail store that is known not only for the quality of its sales and service, but also for the savvy advice that Gand employees share with their customers. He talks about a career path that not many artists or musicians consider when they are starting off: music retailing. As you'll see, it can provide a stable financial base that still allows you to follow your musical dreams while managing to pay the rent.

Joan has been a pianist since the age of five and studied electronic music at Northwestern University. She manages the operations of the store as well as advertising, catalog production, purchasing, and the Gand Web site. Gary has served as a Director of the National Association of Music Merchandisers (NAMM), and is a Syn-Aud-Con graduate. Gary still finds time to go out to do live sound—not just to keep current on the latest technologies, but because he genuinely enjoys helping entertain a coliseum full of people. Joan and Gary's enthusiasm and passion for the music business is infectious to all who have the good fortune to work with them.

Keith: When did you and Joan start the business?

Gary: I started in 1971, with the keyboardist in my band at the time, who is my wife, Joan. We met in high school and we've been together ever since.

K: Unlike the trend towards chain music stores, you operate one retail location.

G: Right, one location, one store. We call ourselves the last of the independents.

Our strategy has always been to have one superstore rather than a bunch of less-than-super stores. Rather than spreading yourself too thin, we decided to take the approach that we were going to keep the one location that we've grown in. And put all our eggs in one basket.

K: How many employees do you have?

G: Right now we've got about twenty-five. Plus a lot of independent engineers and technicians, fix-it guys, consultants—whomever it takes to keep things rolling.

K: What drew you to music, the recording side of things initially?

G: Like a lot of kids, I saw the Beatles on Ed Sullivan when I was about ten years old. I wanted to play music. The whole folk boom was happening at the time in the early 1960s. My dad was a musician in college, a trumpet player. He bought my mother a guitar during the folk days. When she hung it on the wall, he immediately took it down to the basement and started to figure out how to play it.

And literally within hours I was down there asking, so what's going on down here? And my dad showed me how to play it.

Then my sister came down to see what we were doing, and within a few months we had a group, The Gand Family Singers. We started playing local coffee houses and Boy Scout meetings, that kind of stuff.

K: It sounds as if the influence of music around your home played a big role.

G: My dad had a big band in college. My mom was a fan. So there was always music in our house. The radio was always on. I mean I used to fall asleep every night listening to classical music.

We saw a lot of music when I was a kid. My parents took me to see everybody: Segovia, Ravi Shankar, Jimi Hendrix, the Beatles, Frank Zappa, Cream, to name just a few.

And then eventually we got into the family station wagon and headed out on the road. We played all the folk festivals. Played the University of Chicago and Berkeley, all the fiddle festivals down south, Disneyland, and television appearances.

When I got to be a teenager, I started playing rock 'n' roll. I was a banjo player, playing bluegrass. So I switched over to electric guitar. And that got me in front of a different audience. At the same time, we did some tape recordings with our folk trio. And you know, you go into a studio, which at that time was literally two microphones and a tape machine in somebody's closet.

But later, by the time I was really playing electric guitar, things had developed beyond the Beatles' *Sgt. Pepper's* and *Tommy* [by The Who]. You know, the real recording revolution had started. So by the time I got into the studio with my own bands when I was a teenager, we were already recording to eight tracks.

I grew up being a technical person; the kid that was always building model planes and taking the family record player apart and putting it back together. I couldn't help but want to be on the other side of the glass [in the control room] while things were going on. I took a really active role in recording sessions. You know, we'd run through a take and then I'd run on the other side of the glass and I would watch the engineer cue it up. I was fascinated by exactly what he was doing and why.

I would ask, "How are you getting that sound on the snare drum?" I learned most of it firsthand.

And then I did studio work [as a session musician] for a long time, to supplement my music income.

K: I did that, too.

G: Yeah, I played on commercials—a *lot* of beer commercials.

When I got to be eighteen, I was playing at night and doing session work in the daytime. And that's when I decided to open the store. I was doing a lot of repair work and buying guitars at pawnshops and fixing them up and re-selling them for a profit. I needed somewhere to do it. So I opened a small office above a shoe store, which over the years grew into this 10,000-square-foot business.

K: And you met Joan somewhere along the way—was she in the band?

G: Right. About this time, Joan started playing in the band. She was a keyboard player and she also played mandolin. She was playing mandolin a little bit with the folk group, and then she was playing keyboards in our fusion band. She was doing some session work, too, at the same time.

I asked her to do some bookkeeping for the store, and she was also going to college.

K: I guess you might describe Joan's activities as multi-tasking, before the word was even in our vocabulary.

G: Yeah, it didn't exist yet. She was studying electronic music at Northwestern University. That was the year they opened an electronic music lab, so although I wasn't enrolled there—I went to college there. *[Laughs.]* I used to sit in on her classes, and I worked in their electronic music studio there, kind of on the "QT," at night. You know, to learn all about synthesis, and multitrack recording firsthand.

K: So you and Joan really started early.

G: Yeah, we started early, and I've got to say, for a lot of people, to be successful in the music industry, you have to get into it early. I think it's something you have to be into firmly by the time you're a teenager. It's really not something that you get out of college and say: "You know, I think I'd like to be in the music industry." It's got to be in your blood. I think that's a trait of anybody who is successful in anything.

If you look at kids who are good at sports, you find out that they started playing when they were five years old. They've always been into hockey or riding horses or whatever it is.

K: Can you describe your first paying gig?

G: My first paying job in the music business was actually a duo; it was me and my dad playing a Cub Scout meeting. I think we probably made somewhere in the two-figure range. *[Laughs.]* Maybe $10.

K: Have you had any formal training or education that's proven helpful during the years you've been toiling away?

G: Well, I took a De Vry electronics course in high school. I was a little bit of an outcast because I was a vegetarian and had really long hair, which at the time wasn't allowed.

So I took a lot of shop classes and tried to avoid the mainstream. But I did take this De Vry course, which was real early in the morning. That was a really good class for me. I learned all about tubes and transistors.

K: Basics. Stuff that sticks with you all along.

G: Yeah, and I took mechanical drawing, which was a great course because later on when I was working in the studio environment—it was all about block diagrams. Signal flow and learning to read schematics. Understanding patch bays and wiring. Mechanical drawing and the electronics course helped me put it together in my mind.

I would say, any kind of science and math courses you can take…do it.

K: They're going to help you.

G: Yeah, and the other thing is, studying electronic music in the early 1970s, at that time it was all done with patch cords. It was all monophonic.

And that was an incredible learning experience because that really prepared me for everything that came along later on in the studio world. Understanding equalizers and filters…

K: All the things that we use.

G: This is all pre-DSP (digital signal processing), so everything was right in front of you. Now, when you look at a synth, it's all buried menus. And you really don't know what's going on inside there.

K: Until you dig down and do some analysis.

G: Which most people don't do anymore because it just takes too much time.

K: They get a few cool sounds and they stick with them.

G: But I actually had to build these sounds from scratch, so I had a very intimate understanding of the signal flow and how the filters worked and how you modify a sound with an envelope generator and voltage control.

K: Let's talk a little bit about what happens in a typical day or an atypical day at Gand Music & Sound.

G: One of the things that we did when we started the store is we chose our hours around musicians' hours. So we open at noon. And we're open until 8 p.m.—seven days a week.

There's no point in this being a 9-to-5 kind of situation because musicians don't work from 9 to 5. So we really tailored ourselves to ourselves. I mean we were musicians, we were players, and all of our original customers, a lot of whom are still shopping here, were working musicians.

Yeah, so whatever business you're in, you should tailor it to your customer.

But a typical day here is we get in about 11:30, pick up our voice mail, and get the store in shape. We clean up whatever is left over from the night before, vacuum. We check all the displays and make sure everything is still programmed from yesterday. At noon the pandemonium starts. We open the door and it just flows in.

We've got twenty phones lines and they all light up. People come pouring in the front door. We bat balls all day long.

You know, it's exciting. There's never a dull moment here. We've got a constant stream of new gear coming in all the time because we basically built our reputation on being the high-tech guys.

Every day we're getting some kind of new product in here. Most of which doesn't work. *[Laughs.]*

K: So your staff has to figure out how to make some of the gear work.

G: Yeah, they figure out how to make it work and where the bugs are. And what the "work-arounds" are. We then advise our customers accordingly.

K: Yeah, you probably sometimes advise the manufacturers, too, I would guess.

G: A lot of times, yeah. As many times as that happens, and as used to it as you try to get, it's still frustrating. You know, gear is frustrating. But at the same time, if you can master it, the results are incredible.

K: As far as day-to-day job responsibilities, you are involved in just about every aspect of the business, correct?

G: Yes, I'm constantly searching for new products. I talk to manufacturers about things that I would like to see happen. Things that need to happen with products that they already have on the market.

I also handle a lot of the publicity, perfecting the image that Gand has. I make sure our name is out there. I write releases for the magazines, and our Web site. I enjoy writing.

K: Yes, it's another creative outlet.

G: Right, it's like another aspect of performing. If you are a musician, you can communicate in so many ways. You can write lyrics, you can play music, you can do things journalistically, you can do album cover layout, you can do album notes, and you can write product reviews.

K: What's your favorite aspect of your job?

G: Simple—the gear.

K: The gear?

G: I mean I'm a gear-head. I just love gear, equipment, and technology. Gear is cool.

I'm still a very hands-on guy. I mean there's nothing better for me than somebody coming in to the store and saying, "You know, I just built this rack and I'm having all these problems." I'm raring' to go at it, so I'll say, "Let's see what it will take to get it working right." Get rid of ground loops. Figure out why only one channel works. Rip the top off of a piece of gear and see what's going on inside of it.

K: So if a musician walks in and he says, "I can't figure this thing out," you're not up in an ivory tower somewhere, looking at spreadsheets all day?

G: No, definitely not.

K: You're actually down on the floor where the action is?

G: Well, I do spend part of my time analyzing our business and our performance, so I do a good deal of looking at spreadsheets, but if I get a whiff of what is happening on the floor and I can get involved, I will.

If I have information I can share, I will. Because there's a lot of people in this industry that have shared their knowledge with me. There is so much of it that it's a lot easier now. So much of it is available in magazines and online. But when I started, there was none of that.

K: You had to go talk to somebody.

G: There were no vintage guitar books, no recording handbooks, or schools—none of that stuff. I had to talk to the guys in person and learned a lot that way. One of the most important things you can do if you have knowledge is share it with others.

K: Let's talk about somebody who starts off at your store—it's his or her first day. Who are they? What kind of a background do they have? Are they a musician?

G: Well, a lot of the kids that we have that start here are Columbia grads, from Columbia College [in Chicago], which is the big broadcasting and recording college.

Many of them intern here. We're part of Columbia's intern program. And then after they've interned here for a while and they learn the ropes and learn our computer system and everything, I just tell them point blank: when you graduate come and see me. And many do.

I'd say probably a quarter, maybe as much as 33 percent of the people we have here are Columbia grads.

If you want to get into the business, if you can get yourself aligned with a good school that has an intern program with a local studio or local store or whatever—that's a great way to get into the business. Test it out and see which part of it you like.

Some of the guys work for our sound company and they go on the road. Some of the guys are sales people here. Some of the guys work for our install division. There are all different outlets. And also, we have a lot of women working here in management positions, not secretarial positions. It's a good place for women to get a job too. I think the music industry offers good opportunities for women.

K: I do, too.

G: Generally we start people here at the front counter, just so they can learn people's faces and learn how to meet and greet, and get familiar with our regular customers.

And then depending on where their talents may lie, that's kind of the incubation period. Then we like to get them into a department. We're departmentalized here, like a department store.

We have a guitar department, we have a keyboard and synth department, we have a software department, we have a recording department, and we have a PA department. Each one specialized, so that the people in that department are extremely knowledgeable, instead of one guy who knows a little bit about a bunch of things in a store.

And having done all of those jobs myself, I know how hard it is to do them all well. It's better for the customer if they can speak with a specialist. That's how we do it.

Whatever inclination you show being at the front counter, that is generally where we'll put you. What is interesting is our store manager came in as a keyboard salesman. At the time, we didn't need a keyboard salesman. We needed a recording salesman. And we told him that. He says okay, so I'll be a recording salesman. He was able to adapt. So many times a guy will come in with one thing in mind, but there will be a job opening somewhere else. You have to remain flexible.

K: Could you name a few key attributes or skills for an entry-level person?

G: The number one thing we're looking for is a good personality. When we say a good personality, we like someone who is friendly and outgoing, because you can't teach somebody that. We can teach you the technical side of the equipment, but we can't teach you how to be friendly.

Then the next thing is, you need to have some kind of knowledge of the audio world. That may be as limited as having a huge record collection, or it may be as extensive as being a software programmer. It may be having worked in a studio, or being on the concert committee in college. If you don't have a clue about music and you just like music, that's not enough.

Now, interestingly enough, our keyboard salesman right now is a classically trained clarinetist, and we don't sell clarinets or band instruments. Everything that is sold here is electric, with the exception of acoustic guitars. He's an incredible musician, a smart guy, and he likes people. It doesn't matter that the keyboard isn't his favorite instrument.

In fact, for about ten years, we've had a woman who was our lead guitar salesperson, and she doesn't play a lick of guitar. But she knows everything there is to know about a guitar and knows how to make the customer comfortable when she's showing them. If you want to talk shop, she's your person. If you want to jam, then hey, you're on your own.

The other thing about the music business that I find helpful is that appearance is basically meaningless. If you are concerned with your appearance, or if you have the kind of appearance that makes it difficult to get a job in the mall…

K: Come and see us?

G: Come and see us, yeah. [Laughs.] We've got people here with green hair, pierced everything, and lots of tattoos. And they're waiting on customers who may be rappers with baggy clothes, or a woman in diamonds and an evening gown. Individuality is a natural part of the music world.

K: How about the salary range for an entry-level position?

G: We start people out in the $400-a-week range, about $10 an hour. Plus, health insurance kicks in after six months' employment—once we know you are here for a while, and then we put you on. We also offer bonuses and incentives based on performance. So a sales person here that's got a few years of experience, good on the phone, and keeps in touch with their customers and does a lot of follow-up work, you know, can make some serious money.

K: That's great. You mentioned earlier that you do have an internship program, a relationship with Columbia College there. Is it paid or unpaid?

G: That's unpaid. The school won't let you pay their students, but they do receive college credit.

K: How long does it normally last?

G: It usually goes for a quarter. Sometimes it will go for two quarters, depending on…

K: What they have got going?

G: Yeah, what they have got going and what the school has going. Usually what I find is somebody will come and work here for a quarter or two. They'll work at a studio for a quarter or two and then they are working somewhere else music- or broadcast-related. Maybe they will work at an entertainment agency, radio station, or they will work in a record store, or something like that.

K: Do you review them at the conclusion of their internship with Gand?

G: Yes, we do give them an evaluation and I think it's important that they get credit for it. Because what's the point? I mean the experience is wonderful, but…

K: They should get the college credit, too.

G: The other thing that comes from that for us, an internship gives us a peek into what this person is all about. If and when they come back and apply for a job, we've already got a pretty good idea what they are good at and if they'll be able to contribute.

K: Are there any tips you can share for somebody wanting to get into the business?

G: Well, you need experience. Jimi [Hendrix] said it best, "Are you experienced?" And when somebody comes in to work in any of the divisions of our company, that's one of the first things I want to know, once they pass the rest of the tests. I want to know if they are friendly and if they have got a car. You have got to have a car to be able to get to work. And you've got to be punctual. People that show up late or drag their feet, forget it.

You know, something that I learned being in concert audio for all that time is, you have to be on time. It is probably something that doesn't get stressed enough. One of my sayings is, It's impossible to be on time—you are either early or you are late. If you could get to the rest of your life about ten or fifteen minutes early, good things will happen to you.

K: It's true.

G: There's a lot of other basic stuff. One is to tell the truth. If you need some time off work to go play a gig, don't call in sick. Just say, "I have this audition," or "These guys are coming to see my band," or whatever it is. Be up-front about it, because it is more important to be honest than anything else. Trust is such a huge thing. And once you break that, there's no way to repair it. Once you lose somebody's trust you can't get it back.

K: It's fragile.

G: I think another thing that's important in the music industry, on any side of it, is you have to be able to shift gears quickly. This is something that they can't teach in school. You have to be able to just sit there and wait with absolutely nothing happening. And then "BOOM!" The bell rings, the band shows up, and you've got to go full speed. Zero-to-100 in three seconds.

K: Are there any resources that you would recommend?

G: Well, if you can't get experience firsthand, get it by reading about it. There are so many great resources now with all of the magazines. I mean they are all good. Even if you only read one or two of them regularly.

But the best thing to do is to go to gigs. Go to the studio and hang around. Go down to the local club and hang around. Befriend somebody at one of the local concert halls, like one of the stagehands or somebody that can get you in. So you can come in the afternoon and watch the band set up.

When I was a kid, my dad said to me Saturday, "The circus is in town. We can do one of two things. We can go see the circus show tonight. Or we can go over there right now and watch them set up. Which would you like to do?"

I said, "Let's go watch them set up." I'd much rather watch them set up, build the tent, put the stand together, meet the animals, see the clowns. All of that stuff.

To actually watch these guys put it together just fascinated me. So I think, whatever aspect of the business you want to be in, go hang out and watch somebody else do it.

K: What about long-term career prospects? Obviously there has been a lot of pressure over the last few years on music retailers, with the advent of large catalog retailers. And now we've got these immense chains of super stores—Internet music stores are getting launched. If somebody wants to earn a decent living, what's your take…is retail a good choice?

G: Retail is a great choice. It's a great place to be because…year after year after year, there are more retail music sales. The growth is very consistent. There are more people into music, and they are buying more stuff. There is more stuff on the market that they want. When I started out in 1971, I was just selling vintage guitars. They stopped making old equipment a long time ago and I'm still in business. *[Laughs.]* How about that?

So we branched out and started selling new equipment. And then we started selling PA equipment. And then they invented the synthesizer. And then everybody wanted to record themselves. Then there was the drum machine. And then there was the sampler. And then we started selling computers. We were the first Apple Macintosh music dealer back in the 1980s. There's always new stuff.

Now there's MP3. Everybody is burning their own CDs. It's fantastic. And it is not going to stop. The fact is, everybody wants to be entertained. They always did. I mean they used to feed people to the lions and call it entertainment.

So we're still going to see the same thing. They call it the World Wrestling Federation now. People love to experience "the big gig."

For me, I still have a client that I go out and do concert sound gigs for six times a year. It's a complete briefcase gig. No schlepping gear. It keeps me current, but at the same time, it's the same thrill that I had going to the circus with my dad. I mean you go into a huge ice arena with nothing in it. Eight hours later you're throwing a big party for 20,000 people.

The audience comes in and the show starts, and they get that look on their face, you know, they're awestruck.

And then eight hours later, you are gone, like a gypsy. You disappear into the night. It was just a magical dream.

K: That's a great analogy. Are there any parting words of wisdom if you want to have a fulfilling career?

G: I think the most important thing is whatever you do, in the music industry, any industry, whatever job you're in: always do the best job you can whether you are making donuts at Krispy Kreme or setting up mic stands at the local studio.

Do the absolute best job you can at what you're doing now, because it shows. And you should derive satisfaction with that, even if the job is menial. And that trains you for "the big gig." Whatever it turns out to be.

And it takes discipline and practice to make it in the music business. Remember, you need to be pushed in order to grow. And the only way to grow is to continuously challenge yourself. ⊙

An Interview with Gregg Hildebrandt
Northern California Sales Representative for TASCAM Division of TEAC of America

If you want to learn about the latest developments in recording technology, there's no better source than Gregg Hildebrandt. In his more than twenty years in the industry he's been involved in a number of revolutions, such as the move from tube to solid state electronics, from analog to digital, and many others. During his sixteen-year tenure at TASCAM, a name synonymous with the evolution of recording in America, he has been a product manager, clinician, division manager, and regional sales rep.

Although he modestly admits to little or no musical ability, his interpersonal skills and knowledge of recording technology have made him a respected industry resource. Gregg recently left TASCAM's U.S. headquarters, where he had been division manager, to get back to his first love, working directly one-on-one with dealers and customers, listening to their needs, and helping them develop solutions with TASCAM technology.

Keith: Initially, Gregg, what drew you to music?

Gregg: Actually, it was kind of by accident. I was going to college at Fresno State at the time, and working on a major in electronic engineering and a minor in computer science.

I got a job working in a music store in Fresno fixing guitar amplifiers, because at that time solid state amplifiers had just hit the scene. So a lot of companies were coming out with solid state guitar amplifiers. That's how I ended up in the music business.

K: You knew which type of transistor did what, in other words?

G: Yeah, because it was a unique time, right at the end of the tube technology–era and the beginning of solid state. At the time, Kustom had just come out with a line of guitar amplifiers and so the music store that I worked for in Fresno was the Kustom dealer. And of course, they had a lifetime guarantee. So since solid state was not as stable as it is now—you could say it kept me pretty busy. *[Laughs.]*

K: You mentioned you were studying electronics and computers at Fresno State. Did that help your career?

G: To be perfectly blunt, neither the electronics background nor the computer science background has really helped that much, long term. Those technologies were developing so rapidly, frankly, they evolved way past what I had learned within a matter of two or three years.

The formal training that's been the most helpful to me, believe it or not, is various sales training and sales seminars. I have always been fascinated with just the theory of selling because it requires convincing people to your way of thinking.

K: Did you have any early mentors?

G: Absolutely. My first job was at a music store called Sound Stage in Fresno. As a matter of fact, that store still exists. The Spitzer family owns it now, but at the time Bob and Camille Wilson owned it. Bob Wilson was really my biggest early mentor. Because again, I had no music background whatsoever—just a technical background.

Bob came to me one day and said, "You know, you are pretty good talking with customers. Why don't you become a salesman and sell things for me?" And I said, "Gee Bob, I could never be a salesman." Because at that time, my impression of what a salesman was—what most people's impression is—a used-car type of salesman. You know, with white shoes and a white belt. [Laughs.]

And Bob said, "No, all you really need to do is just explain the products to people. And if it's the right product...they will buy it."

And I answered, "But I'm not a musician, I don't know anything about this type of equipment."

Then he asked me, "Well, I tell you what, what *are* you really interested in?" I told him that I liked hi-fi and stereo equipment. So he said, "Well, that's great. Why don't we open up a little stereo section here and why don't you pick a few lines, and get started selling hi-fi equipment? Okay?"

So we did that, and of course it was about six months later that I kind of evolved into learning more and more about musical instruments and started selling musical instruments.

He saw something in me and really got me started in the business and was very much of a guiding hand the first several years. He actually made me a store manager and then a branch manager as well.

K: It sounds as if there are two key points worth emphasizing regarding your start. The first is that, for people to excel, they have to work on something that they are enthusiastic about.

G: That's exactly right.

K: So Bob knew that and put it to good use to get you into selling. He likely knew that long term, he wasn't going to be a hi-fi dealer. The second point is that often the toughest part of selling, especially for someone who is new to sales, is demolishing their mental image of the pushy used-car salesman.

G: Yes, the myth that all sales people have to be high-pressure types. To this day, I find that really, it is just explaining the concept clearly and concisely, and then listening to what the customer has to say.

Bob Wilson actually taught me to be a pretty decent guitar salesman, even though I couldn't even tune a guitar at the time. Simply because other stores would hire hot guitar players to sell guitars, and of course when somebody comes in, and the salesman pulls a guitar down and starts wailing on it—there's a real intimidation...

K: The customer promptly walks out the door.

G: Yes. And with me, I didn't have that option. I would put the guitar in their hands *[laughs]*...and beg them, "Do something with it... please."

K: That's so true. You mentioned earlier, you're currently representing TASCAM products throughout Northern California. So that means you are calling on...

G: Music stores...everything from small music stores to pro audio accounts, to film facilities like Skywalker, Saul Zaentz, and Zoetrope film centers. Because TASCAM has such a broad line of recording products, I also call on sound contractors and a few broadcast accounts as well.

Before that, I was division manager of TASCAM for eight years, and I lived in Los Angeles. Frankly, that's life in the fast lane. After a certain amount of time, it became pretty obvious that I was ready for a change; I needed to kind of slow down a little bit.

I was fortunate because my boss knew that I had always wanted to move back home to Northern California, where I was born and raised. He suggested, "Why don't you open up a sales office for us up there?" So I did. I'm back out with customers and I love it.

I work with a wide variety of different users, with different applications and different levels of experiences and expertise: everything from a guitar player who is trying to buy his first mini-studio, up through Skywalker Sound, which is trying to figure out how to cram as much audio information over a high-speed network as possible while they build the next blockbuster movie soundtrack.

K: What's the ratio of time you spend out in the field versus your home office?

G: Well, I typically try and spend one day a week in my home office, and that's generally on Monday. And then I spend the rest of the week out in the field, because frankly that's the part of the job that I enjoy the most—getting a chance to work with people, doing sales training and product training. I also like talking to some of the higher-end-users that are trying to figure out how to push that envelope a little bit.

K: So you're helping people get the most out of the latest products and technologies, and training retailers to understand and educate their end-users about how TASCAM products work.

G: Yes, but the part of the job that is still the most fun, believe it or not, is when you are talking to somebody who has never done any recording before. I like to go through the basics of how multitrack works and what that can do to expand their fun. You will see their eyes light up when they realize the possibilities, and that new-found sense of discovery. It's really something.

K: Could you describe an entry-level position at TASCAM?

G: TASCAM is a manufacturer and a distributor of recording products in the U. S. What most people would probably think of as entry-level would probably be at our headquarters in Los Angeles for order entry and things like that.

But what I would consider more of an entry-level position from a sales standpoint would be a sales rep position. Essentially that would be going out and calling on end-users and dealers on a regular basis.

K: Could you identify some of the key skills for someone getting started in the sales end of the business?

G: Absolutely. I think number one, they need to be "people" person, somebody that enjoys talking and listening to people. Because far and away the easiest way to sell a person something is to get them talking, and then listen. Which is just so much easier if you have a genuine interest in people.

Number two, a person has got to be very self-motivated. It isn't a 9-to-5 job when you are out in the field doing sales. There isn't a supervisor looking over your shoulder every step of the way. So you must be self-motivated and understand that your time is your most valuable asset.

And then three, I think it helps to be pretty well organized, because frankly, when you are a sales rep, you run an independent branch office. You basically are doing everything from paperwork to dealer mailings, and putting together material for trade shows, clinics, and presentations.

Organizational skills ensure that every effort you put out pays off in the greatest number of ways. That's critically important.

K: What would be the salary range for a rookie sales rep?

G: It again depends entirely on the territories, but probably in the \$36,000- to \$48,000-a-year range, including both base salary and commission.

K: Is there any type of internship program at TASCAM's home office in Los Angeles?

G: We have just started hiring interns within the TASCAM division. The corporate office has done some internship programs, more from a business administration standpoint.

One of the things we recently discovered is that a great deal of the schools require an internship in order to earn a degree. So one of the things that we have started doing within the last year is to bring on some interns, as an experiment. And as a matter of fact, I am going to be getting one soon here in Northern California.

K: How has the experiment gone so far?

G: We have had one in Phoenix, working with our regional sales manager now for about six months. And the experience has been very, very good because it allows somebody to get out, work with some of the dealers, and find out if they really do want to do this type of work as a career. In fact, the person that was working with our regional in Phoenix was just hired by one of our dealers upon graduation.

K: Is the internship a paid or unpaid position?

G: It's unpaid, because the schools require it to be an unpaid position. However, we do cover an intern's expenses for gas, phones, copies, and what have you.

K: How long does the internship run?

G: They are typically positions that are designed to be six months to a year in duration. Just enough time to expose them to the realities of a sales position, while also getting exposure to some potential employers.

K: Do you have any tips for someone starting out to get their foot in the door?

G: Well, the biggest tip that I would offer would be to take your time and pay your dues. Upon graduation, an awful lot of people expect to start off with a high-paying, high-visibility job. Very few people actually do. So I think to be successful with a company, you need to work your way up. You need to have a very broad background. I would suggest someone get a position in a fairly small music retail environment, where you have the opportunity to wear a lot of different hats.

They should learn about many different products, because in that environment, you need to. That doesn't mean that getting a sales position in a bigger retail establishment isn't good. But you don't quite have the opportunity to experience some of the things like going to the bank in the morning or dealing with the UPS driver.

K: That's right. Or sweeping up the store after a clinic.

G: Exactly, or making sure that you sent out the invitations to the clinic, those type of things which, frankly, they seem real basic, but until you have an opportunity to make some mistakes, you don't realize how important the little details are.

You should get an entry-level position where you're going to get the broadest exposure to the realities of what you've got to do. In our industry in particular, very seldom do you end up in a position where you have a large staff to do all the different functions. Even when I was division manager of TASCAM, everyone in management wore a whole bunch of different hats.

K: Are there any magazines, books, or trade associations that you would recommend as resources?

G: Trade magazines such as *Mix*, *EQ*, and *Pro Sound News* are very good. There's an awful lot of information on the Internet. Just start searching for things that interest you. You will be amazed at how much information you can find. But subscribing to two or three of the industry magazines makes the most sense, because that will really give you a good feel for what's going on.

The other thing that I would recommend for anyone going out on an interview would be to take the time to learn a little bit about the company you're interviewing at. You'd be amazed at how many people show up for a job interview, and don't have any idea whatsoever of what the company that they're trying to get a job with actually *does*!

It's impressive when somebody does come in for an interview and obviously they have taken the time to read a couple of catalogs or brochures. That really sets them apart from the great unwashed that are just trying to get a job.

K: What's your long-term view as far as careers in the music, recording, or entertainment business?

G: I think they are excellent. They are evolving quite a bit, but I think they're particularly good from a sales and a product standpoint.

Let's face it, in the best or worst of times, entertainment and music have always tended to thrive, because it's something that everybody enjoys in one form or another, whether it's performing or listening to…or participating in, in some form or another.

For instance, if someone is buying an instrument, there needs to be a nice fit between the type of instrument, its cost, and their level of playing. Are they a beginner or a player with lots of experience? And so that's where the expertise of a salesperson really pays off.

Just like in the clothing business. Let's face it: I can't imagine buying a suit over the Internet. It's the same thing with musical instruments and recording equipment. People still want to have them in their hands and feel them and touch them and listen to them. That keeps our long-term prospects I think very, very good for the industry.

K: Do you have any tips on market segments you think that will be particularly hot in the future?

G: Yes, absolutely. I think that it's going to be the nontraditional users. In the past, when I got started in this business, pretty much whether you were selling musical instruments or recording equipment, we had a very limited potential audience. I mean the only reason somebody would want to record multitrack music would be if they were a professional musician.

Now, with a lot of the computer-based software packages and sequencers, and a whole range of affordable instruments and recording tools, we've broadened the potential user base significantly. Plus the pricing of technology keeps coming down, so that people can do everything from taking home movies and putting them into the computer, then adding sound tracks to them, and things like that.

I think it's going to be these types of nontraditional users, the non-hard-core musician, who represent a huge market. This group will be absolutely booming in the future.

K: Do you have any parting words of wisdom?

G: The music business is totally a people-oriented business. It's not something that can be easily faked. And frankly, you will be as successful as the relationships you build over the years. Care about what you do, how you do it, and the people you work with. The rest will come to you. ⦿

appendices

Author's Career Path

Keith Hatschek,
President of Keith Hatschek & Associates

What follows is a brief look at Keith Hatschek's career in the music and recording industry. You will find it illustrative of the themes and principles that have been outlined throughout the book. His career path took a number of unplanned turns, gradually leading him to his current position.

I came to California in 1965 from North Carolina as a teenager. I grabbed onto the first thing that interested me in my new environment: music.

My family arrived in the Golden State just before school adjourned for the summer. It was just kismet that people up the street had a band. The boy who had been playing bass moved away and there was no one to fill in. After the guys checked me out for a few days they said, "Well, if he has a skateboard, he can't be *too* weird." They came to my house and said, "Look, anyone can play the bass, it's only got four strings. Why don't you come on over here, and we'll try to show you how to play it."

As a teenager, I had scored—social interaction! It helped that I grew up listening to music. My parents listened to the radio and records and my dad played the piano when he was young.

So I started to play the bass, and of course the cool thing was that when we practiced, girls stood outside of the garage. So right away, I knew there was definitely an opportunity here for something beyond just blisters on my teenage fingers.

I took to playing music. I loved it. The two things I liked the most were the interaction with other musicians and the mathematical nature of music. If you've ever arranged or composed music, you know there's a very close relationship between mathematics and music, in terms of how the elements fit together—a symmetry.

Although I'm no longer involved in playing or writing music, my kids recently made me get my guitar out, re-string it, and buy an amp. I strum on it a little bit these days while they play the piano.

I loved music. I loved sound. I continued playing in bands. By the time I was in eleventh grade we were getting paid $300 a night to play at dances. It was big money in the 1960s. Wow, $300. My share seemed like gas money for the rest of my life!

So from there I went to college at the University of California, Riverside, and for one year I was in the music program and I was doing great. The dean of the music department, "Doctor Don," encouraged every student with an interest in music to pursue his or her musical dreams. Doctor Don used in play in Paul Whiteman's orchestra during the heyday of the big bands.

His belief was, as long as people are listening to music and their toes are tapping, then you're learning. So I was playing in a jazz ensemble, learning how to write four-part harmony, and studying theory. However, I wanted to be close to my friends, so I transferred to the University of California campus at Berkeley, with enough credits to be a junior. I immediately flunked out of every aptitude test you take to make sure that you are really a junior in the music program.

When I went to do my interview, my instrument was the jazz guitar, leading the teacher to ask, where was my "real" guitar? I said, "Well, this is a real guitar, it has six strings—there's my music and here is my audition tape."

He replied, "I'm sorry, you'll have to go down to the basement at the student union where the pep band plays, and that's not for credit. You will have to start over as a freshman with a recognized instrument.

So ended my collegiate music performance education. I switched gears and earned a degree in history, just to basically escape college with a degree. And I kept playing in rock bands. I had a band in the Bay Area in 1970s. We eventually secured a development deal with Capitol Records. Unfortunately, they found out after we recorded three songs that no one wanted to play us on the radio. That introduced me painfully to the harsh reality of the record business. In the 1970s, if your song wasn't on the radio, you (and your record label) didn't make any money.

I was playing a jingle one night in San Mateo, California, at a now defunct studio. The engineer fell asleep at the mixing board during a take. We were done playing and we said, "Play it back." Musicians are in one room, the studio, and the engineer is in another room, the control room. We couldn't see the engineer. We were standing up, and we finally went in the control room and the engineer was dead asleep on the mixing board.

That experience changed my perspective. I went home and thought, "If that guy can have a job running a recording studio and he falls asleep on the job, I can do better." Famous last words!

After this experience I visited two legendary studios, Wally Heider's and the Automatt, in San Francisco. I said I want to work in the studio and the managers all said, "Don't do it. Don't do it. Do anything but that."

Undeterred, I thought, "I'll show you guys. I'll build my own recording studio." I was in my twenties—and I knew I could conquer the world. So I built a studio in 1979 in San Carlos, California. Bayshore Studios was born as a rehearsal room for bands, and acquired a TASCAM 3340 4-track, then evolved to an 8-track recorder. I picked up two partners along the way. We bought some more gear, and some more gear, and yes, a bit more gear.

After a few years I got married, and my wife and I started a family. One day I came to the realization, that "Wow, I am working twenty hours a day, seven days a week, and I have a family. Hmm, what am I going to do?"

I decided to close my business and go to work for another studio. A tough decision to make, but in hindsight, it was absolutely the best thing to do. I had done my own apprenticeship to learn the basics of recording and business. Then I had a successful twelve-year run at a studio called the Music Annex, which is still in operation in the Bay Area today. I started as a tape copy room person and engineer for my previous clients.

After a year and a half at Music Annex, I was answering the phones while the regular phone person was out to lunch. While I subbed on the phone, there were more sessions booked. The owner of the studio thought, "Hmm, maybe there's an opportunity here. Every time Hatschek is on the phone our bookings increase. So if I put him on the phone all day, think how much time we could book?!"

So he made me an offer. "I'm paying you this much as an engineer and you're not working all the time. [Beginning engineers seldom are in session all day.] I'll pay you a bit more to work in studio management selling studio time and to come up with ideas so that we can hustle some more business." And I said, "Okay, I'll try it."

I still did a few sessions with bands I really liked and for projects I was well suited for. I got more involved in planning and studio management. Business increased. Music Annex opened two new divisions to develop a market for audio post production in 1984 and for cassette and CD duplication in 1986. Business increased some more. The company was profitable and my earnings rode the crest of the company's growth. I got promoted. I got promoted again. By now, not engineering sessions didn't faze me because I was stimulated and challenged by helping to grow a successful multimillion-dollar studio business.

One of the prime products was the duplication of audio cassettes with music and spoken-word programming. It was a great business. The company did very well through the 1980s and early 1990s, and then pretty soon people started saying, "Yeah, I think I'll just put my record out on a CD. I don't need a cassette."

I went to the owner and suggested that we should consider the sale of that division of the company. That was the division I spent most of my time managing. The owners agreed and after about a year, we located a buyer. And once the sale was formalized, it hit me, "Wow, the company is selling this division! It's really happening. All those people are going to report to another person, not to me anymore."

It became clear that I needed to find something else to do. That's when I came up with the idea of starting my own consulting practice. That happened in 1995. And pretty quickly it grew into a marketing and public relations agency. We specialize in working for companies that are in broadcasting, recording technologies, and the media industries. We help our clients tell their story through press relations, advertisements, direct mail campaigns, and all types of marketing programs to increase their profile and sales.

I've come a long way since sitting in that garage in 1965 learning how to play the bass line to "Gloria." I have developed a broad range of skills, first as a musician, then as a recording engineer, then as a studio manager. Making the jump to the business side of the recording studio game was a break that soon showed me how much I could grow in that area. Then I pursued a tighter focus on marketing, promotion, and advertising for a range of clients around the world.

I have taken the liberty of spending a good bit of time on my career path, because I believe that it is typical of careers in the entertainment industry. Most people come to it with a set of skills and perceptions of what they see themselves doing, but the fact is that at the end of many successful careers, people have jumped tracks a number of times to take advantage of new opportunities. You find a lot of the people in the A&R departments of labels that used to be in bands. You find many engineers that used to either be in a band or work in a music store. You find label presidents that used to be music attorneys. You'll meet personal managers that started as ushers. And many company presidents who on occasion still strum their guitar or blow their horn. ⊙

The author regularly presents career development seminars at recording industry schools around the world. The daylong seminars provide students an up-to-the-minute look at the latest strategies for breaking into the competitive music and recording industry. Each seminar concludes with a VIP panel discussion featuring leaders from the entertainment industry sharing their experience with students.

For more information or to schedule a seminar, send an e-mail request to **info@hatschek.com**.

Selected Resources

Periodicals (many have online editions)

Billboard

Mix

Pro Sound News

Electronic Musician

EQ

A/V Video

Keyboard

Recording

Gig

Radio & Records

Books

Dannen, Frederic. *Hit Men*. New York: Times Books, 1990.

Field, Shelly. *Career Opportunities in the Music Industry, 3rd edition*. New York: Facts on File, 1995.

Half, Robert. *How to Get a Better Job in This Crazy World*. New York: Plume, 1991.

Kimpel, Dan. *Networking in the Music Business*. Cincinnati, Ohio: Writer's Digest Books, 1993.

Olsen, Eric, Paul Verna, and Carla Wolff. *The Encyclopedia of Record Producers*. New York: Watson-Guptill Publishers, 1999.

Passman, Don. *All You Need to Know About the Music Business*. New York: Simon & Schuster, 1994.

Payne, Richard A. *How to Get a Better Job Quicker*. New York: New American Library, 1982.

Stone, Chris. *Audio Recording for Profit*. Woburn, Mass.: Focal Press, 2000.

Industry Biographies

Buskin, Richard. *Inside Tracks: History of Pop Music from the World's Greatest Record Producers*. New York: Spike, 1999.

Copeland, Ian. *Wild Thing: Memoirs of Ian Copeland*. (Out of print, available in many used book stores.)

Dickerson, James. *Women on Top*. New York: Watson-Guptill Publishers, 1998.

Holzman, Jac and Gavan Daws. *Follow the Music*. Santa Monica: First Media Books, 1999.

King, Tom. *The Operator: David Geffen Builds the New Hollywood*. New York: Random House, 2000.

Kooper, Al. *Backstage Passes and Backstabbing Bastards*. New York: Watson-Guptill Publishers, 1998.

Martin, Sir George and Jeremy Hornsby. *All You Need is Ears*. New York: St. Martin's Press, 1995.

Small, Mark and A. Taylor. *Masters of Music*. Boston: Berklee Press, 1999.

Professional Associations

NARAS (National Academy of Recording Arts & Sciences)
National Office: (310) 392-3777
www.grammy.com

SPARS (Society of Professional Audio Recording Services)
National Office: (901) 821-9111
www.spars.com/spars

AES (Audio Engineering Society)
National Office: (212) 661-8528
www.aes.org

A last note...

If you are searching for a book that is out of print, try www.alibris.com, a Web site with a very good search engine to locate out-of-print and hard-to-find books. At the time of writing, every one of the out-of-print works referenced in this book was available there.

Trade Associations

American Music Therapy Association (AMTA)
8455 Colesville Rd., Suite 1000
Silver Spring, MD 20910
(301) 589-3300
www.musictherapy.org

American Choral Directors Association (ACDA)
P.O. Box 6310
Lawton, OK 73506
(405) 355-8161
www.acdaonline.org

American Composers Alliance
170 West 74th Street
New York, NY 10023
(212) 362-8900
www.composers.com

American Federation of Musicians (AFM)
1501 Broadway, Suite 600
New York, NY 10036
(212) 869-1330
www.afm.org

American Society of Composers and Publishers (ASCAP)
1 Lincoln Plaza
New York, NY 10023
(212) 621-6000
www.ascap.com

American Society of Music Arrangers & Composers (ASMA)
P.O. Box 11
Hollywood, CA 90078
(213) 658-5997
www.asmac.org

American Society of Music Copyists (ASMC)
Box 2557
Times Square Station
New York, NY 10108
(212) 586-2140

Broadcast Music, Inc. (BMI)
320 West 57th Street
New York, NY 10019
(212) 586-2000
www.bmi.com

Consumer Electronics Association (CEA)
2500 Wilson Ave.
Arlington, VA 22201
(703) 907-7600
www.ce.org

Country Music Association (CMA)
P.O. Box 22299
One Music Circle South
Nashville, TN 37203
(615) 244-2840
www.countrymusic.org

Electronic Industry Alliance (EIA)
2500 Wilson Ave.
Arlington, VA 22201
(703) 907-7500
www.eia.org

Gospel Music Association (GMA)
P.O. Box 23201
Nashville, TN 37202
(615) 242-0303
www.gospelmusic.org

Music Educators National Conference (MENC)
1806 Robert Fulton Drive
Reston, VA 20191
(703) 860-4000
www.menc.org

Music Publishers Association
PMB 246
1562 First Avenue
New York, NY 10028
(212) 327-4044
www.mpa.org

National Academy of Recording Arts and Sciences (NARAS)
3402 Pico Boulevard
Santa Monica, CA 90405
(310) 392-3777
www.grammy.com

National Association for Campus Activities (NACA)
13 Harbison Way
Columbia, SC 29212-3401
(803) 732-6222
www.naca.org

National Association for Music Therapy, Inc. (NAMT)
8455 Colesville Road, Suite 1000
Silver Spring, MD 20910
(301) 589-3300
www.namt.com

National Association of Broadcast Employees and Technicians (NABET)
7101 Wisconsin Avenue, Suite 800
Bethesda, MD 20814
(301) 657-8420
www.union.nabetcwa.org/nabet

National Association of Broadcasters (NAB)
1771 N Street NW
Washington, DC 20036
(202) 429-5300
www.nab.org

National Association of Music Merchants (NAMM)
5790 Armada Drive
Carlsbad, CA 92008
(619) 438-8001
www.namm.org

National Association of Recording Merchandisers (NARM)
9 Eves Drive, Suite 120
Marlton, NJ 08053
(609) 596-2221
www.narm.com

National Association of Schools of Music (NASM)
11250 Roger Bacon Drive, Suite 21
Reston, VA 20190
(703) 434-0700
www.arts-accredit.org/nasm/nasm.htm

Public Relations Society of America (PRSA)
33 Irving Place
New York, NY 10003
(212) 995-2230
www.prsa.org

Recording Industry Association of America (RIAA)
1020 19th Street NW, Suite 200
Washington, DC 20036
(202) 775-0101
www.riaa.org

SESAC, Inc.
10 Columbus Circle
New York, NY 10019
(212) 586-3450

55 Music Square East
Nashville, TN 37203
www.sesac.com

Society of Professional Audio Recording Studios (SPARS)
364 Clove Drive
Memphis, TN 38117
(901) 821-9111
www.spars.com

The Songwriters Guild
1560 Broadway, Suite #1306
New York, NY 10036
(212) 768-7902

1222 16th Avenue South, Suite 25
Nashville, TN 37212
(615) 329-1782

6430 Sunset Boulevard, Suite 705
Hollywood, CA 90028
(323) 462-1108
www.songwriters.org

Index

Music Business and Reference Books from Berklee Press

As Serious About Music As You Are.

COMPLETE GUIDE TO FILM SCORING
▸ by Richard Davis
Learn the art and business of writing music for films and TV. Topics include: the film-making process, preparing and recording a score, contracts and fees, publishing, royalties, and copyrights. Features interviews with 19 film-scoring professionals.
50449417 Book $24.95

THE CONTEMPORARY SINGER ▸ by Anne Peckham
Maximize your vocal potential by learning how to use and protect your voice properly. Develop stage presence, microphone technique, stamina, range, and sound with exercises for all voice ranges and types on the accompanying CD. Includes lead sheets for such standard vocal repertoire pieces as *Yesterday, I'm Beginning to See the Light,* and *I Heard It Through the Grapevine.*
50449438 Book/CD $24.95

ESSENTIAL EAR TRAINING ▸ by Steve Prosser
Step-by-step introduction to the basics of ear training and sight singing, as taught at Berklee College of Music. Develop your inner ear and musical vocabulary, learn to hear the music you see, understand the music you hear, and notate the music you have composed or arranged. Complete course with rhythmic and melodic studies using conducting patterns.
50449421 Book $14.95

THE NEW MUSIC THERAPIST'S HANDBOOK, SECOND EDITION ▸ by Suzanne B. Hanser
Dr. Hanser's well-respected Music Therapist's Handbook has been thoroughly updated and revised to reflect the latest developments in the field of music therapy. Features an introduction to music therapy, new clinical applications and techniques, case studies, designing, implementing, and evaluating individualized treatment programs, and guidelines for beginning music therapists.
50449424 Book $29.95

HOW TO GET A JOB IN THE MUSIC AND RECORDING INDUSTRY
▸ by Keith Hatschek
The bible for anyone who has ever dreamed of landing a job in the music business, from producing or engineering the next Top 10 hit to running a record company. Featuring advice and secrets to educate and empower the serious music and recording industry job seeker, including: details on booming job prospects in new media, a resource directory of key publications and top industry trade organizations, interviews with pros revealing how they got their start, and networking tips.
50449505 Book $24.95

THE SELF-PROMOTING MUSICIAN
▸ by Peter Spellman
Take charge of your career with crucial do-it-yourself strategies. If you are an independent musician, producer, studio owner, or label, you should own this book! Features tips for writing business plans, creating press kits, using the Internet for promotion, customizing demos and getting music played on college radio, along with a comprehensive musician's resource list.
50449423 Book $24.95

THE MUSICIAN'S INTERNET ▸ by Peter Spellman
Promote your music online! Learn to reach new audiences, expand your online presence, and attract thousands of new fans. A must for any self-managed musician.
50449527 Book..............................$24.95

For more information about Berklee Press or Berklee College of Music, contact us:
1140 Boylston Street ▸ Boston, MA 02215-3693
617-747-2146
www.berkleepress.com

Visit your local music dealer or bookstore, or go to **www.berkleepress.com**

Distributed By

Prices and availability subject to change without notice.

Music Technology and Method Books from Berklee Press

As Serious About Music As You Are.

Prices and availability subject to change without notice.

MUSIC TECHNOLOGY

FINALE: AN EASY GUIDE TO MUSIC NOTATION
▸ by Thomas E. Rudolph and Vincent A. Leonard, Jr.

Finale made easy! *The* indispensable resource for learning to use this most powerful and popular music notation software program. Designed for both novice and experienced Finale users, the easy to follow step-by-step instructions will help you fully understand and master all of Finale's capabilities. Compatible for both Macintosh and Windows computer platforms.

50449501 Book/CD-ROM....................$59.95

PRODUCING IN THE HOME STUDIO WITH PRO TOOLS
▸ by David Franz

Get the most out of Pro Tools by improving your music production skills and engineering techniques. This comprehensive home studio production guide will help songwriters, artists, engineers, and producers create professional-quality recordings using Digidesign's Pro Tools. CD-ROM includes Pro Tools FREE and examples of Pro Tools sessions with audio and MIDI files.

50449526 Book/CD-ROM....................$34.95

RECORDING IN THE DIGITAL WORLD
▸ by Thomas E. Rudolph and Vincent A. Leonard, Jr.

Build the perfect digital studio, no matter what your budget. Includes advice and recommendations on studio equipment, software, and the latest technologies, plus practical tips for creating, editing, and mastering a digital recording.

50449472 Book $29.95

ARRANGING IN THE DIGITAL WORLD
▸ by Corey Allen

Great for beginners! Create truly inspired digital arrangements using today's electronic and digital instruments. Teaches basic sequencing, production concepts, with step-by-step directions for building MIDI arrangements in any style. Also includes a MIDI disk with more than 50 sequenced examples.

50449415 Book/GM Disk....................$19.95

DISTRIBUTED BY HAL•LEONARD®

BERKLEE METHOD

A MODERN METHOD FOR GUITAR
▸ by William Leavitt

Used as the basic text by the Berklee College of Music guitar program, the Leavitt method has stood the test of time and earned legions of loyal followers. Now you can have all three volumes of this classic guitar method in one convenient book. Includes music fundamentals, scales, melodic studies, chord and arpeggio studies, intervals, chord construction and voicings, improvisation, and rhythm guitar technique.

Volumes 123 Complete
50449468 Book....................................$29.95

Also available in separate volumes:

Volume 1: Beginner
50449404 Book/CD $22.95
50449402 Book/Cassette $22.95
50449400 Book only $14.95

Volume 2: Intermediate
50449412 Book/Cassette $22.95
50449410 Book only $14.95

Volume 3: Advanced
50449420 Book....................................$14.95

A MODERN METHOD FOR KEYBOARD
▸ by James Progris

Learn how to sight read, develop technical facility, and sharpen your knowledge of harmonic motion, effective chord voicing, and patterns of contemporary chord progression. Used as the basic text for the Berklee College of Music keyboard program.

Volume 1: Beginner
50449620 Book....................................$14.95

Volume 2: Intermediate
50449630 Book....................................$14.95

Volume 3: Advanced
50449640 Book....................................$14.95

For more information about Berklee Press or Berklee College of Music, contact us:
1140 Boylston Street ▸ Boston, MA 02215-3693
617-747-2146
www.berkleepress.com

Visit your local music dealer or bookstore, or go to **www.berkleepress.com**